To:

_____

From:

_____

TOASTS FOR EVERY OCCASION

Jennifer Rahel Conover

NEW AMERICAN LIBRARY

New American Library
Published by New American Library, a division of
Penguin Group (USA) Inc., 375 Hudson Street,
New York, New York 10014, USA
Penguin Group (Canada), 10 Alcorn Avenue, Toronto,
Ontario M4V 3B2, Canada (a division of Pearson Penguin Canada Inc.)
Penguin Books Ltd., 80 Strand, London WC2R 0RL, England
Penguin Ireland, 25 St. Stephen's Green, Dublin 2,
Ireland (a division of Penguin Books Ltd.)
Penguin Group (Australia), 250 Camberwell Road, Camberwell, Victoria 3124,
Australia (a division of Pearson Australia Group Pty. Ltd.)
Penguin Books India Pvt. Ltd., 11 Community Centre, Panchsheel Park,
New Delhi - 110 017, India
Penguin Group (NZ), cnr Airborne and Rosedale Roads, Albany,
Auckland 1310, New Zealand (a division of Pearson New Zealand Ltd.)
Penguin Books (South Africa) (Pty.) Ltd., 24 Sturdee Avenue,
Rosebank, Johannesburg 2196, South Africa

Penguin Books Ltd., Registered Offices: 80 Strand, London WC2R 0RL, England

First published by New American Library, a division of Penguin Group (USA) Inc.

First Printing, May 2001
19   18   17   16   15   14   13   12

● REGISTERED TRADEMARK—MARCA REGISTRADA

LIBRARY OF CONGRESS CATALOGING-IN-PUBLICATION DATA:

Toasts for every occasion / [compiled by] Jennifer Rahel Conover.
p.   cm.
Includes index.
ISBN 0-451-20301-1
1. Toasts.   I. Conover, Jennifer Rahel.
PN6341.T624 2001
808.5'1—dc21
00-048196

Printed in the United States of America
Set in Simoncini Garamond
Designed by Leonard Telesca

Heartfelt thanks to my husband, Ted, daughter, Rahel, sister, Susie, and to Clare Marlowe, Betty and Pres Northcutt, Kathy and Ray Heimbecker, Annemarie and Michael Victory and Annie Wenner for all their wonderful toasts and never-ending encouragement. My deepest thanks also to my agent, Joyce Flaherty, "who never ever sells me short," and Ellen Edwards, my editor, "who can read me like a book"! Last but in no way least, a very special thanks to Tom Kearns, who never fails to rescue me from all my computer nightmares!

"It was my Uncle George who discovered that alcohol was a food well in advance of medical thought."

—from *The Inimitable Jeeves*
by P. G. Wodehouse

Contents

Introduction   1

How to Use This Book   6

International—To Your Health   9

Similar Toasts from Different Nations   12

Toasts by Category   15

  Absent Friends   15

  Accountants   17

  Action   17

  Actors   18

  Adolescence   19

  Adventure   19

  Advertising   20

  Advice   20

  Age   21

  Agents   27

  Alimony   27

  Ambition   28

  America   28

  Anniversary   30

  Antiques   32

April Fools' Day   32
Architects   33
Athletes   33
Attitude   33
Babies   34
Bachelors and Bachelorettes   37
Bakers   38
Baldness   38
Bankers   39
Beauty   39
Beer and Ale   39
Best Wishes   44
Better Times   45
Birthdays   47
Blacksmiths   49
Blessings   50
Bosses   54
Builders   54
Celebration   55
Celebrities and Well-Known Individuals   55
Challenges   60
Champagne   60
Children   62
Chimney Sweeps   63
Christening   63
Christmas   64
Clans   69
Coaches   70

Congratulations 70

Courage 71

Creativity 72

Creditors 72

Critics 72

Curses 73

Death and the Departed 75

Defeat 79

Dentists 80

Diplomats 81

Discretion 82

Divorce 83

Doctors and Medicine 83

Dreams 84

Drink 84

Drunkenness 92

Editors 94

Enemies 94

Entrepreneurs 95

Eternity 95

Excellence 95

Family 96

Farewells 96

Farmers 97

Fathers 98

Firemen 98

Fishing 99

Focus 101

Food	101
Fourth of July	102
Freedom	103
Friendship	103
Future	114
Gambling	114
Gardening	115
General	115
Generosity	126
Golf	127
Good Fortune	127
Graduate	129
Gratitude	129
Greatness	130
Grocers	130
Guests	130
Hangovers	132
Happiness	132
Hard Times	135
Health	140
Hell	143
Home	145
Hope	146
Hosts	147
Humor	149
Husbands	159
Ideas	160
Imagination	160

Immediacy	160
Ireland	161
Kindness	162
Kiss	163
Lawyers	165
Leadership	166
Life	167
Literary	171
Love	173
Luck	183
Luxury	185
Marriage	185
Men	190
Military	192
Millennium	196
Miners	197
Ministers	198
Miracles	198
Mistakes	198
Moderation	199
Mothers	200
Mountain Man	202
Nature	202
Nautical	202
New Year's	205
Opportunity	207
Optimism	208
Patience	208

Peace   208
Perseverance   209
Philosophy   210
Pilots   210
Politicians   210
Postal Workers   211
Poverty   211
Praise   212
Press   212
Procrastination   213
Professors and Education   213
Prohibition   214
Prosperity   215
Psychiatrists   216
Retirees and Retirement   216
Risk   217
Risqué   217
St. David's Day   229
St. Patrick's Day   230
Salesmen   230
Song   231
Sorrow   232
Speakers   232
Spoonerism   233
Stockbrokers   233
Success   234
Teamwork   236
Tennis   237

Thanksgiving   238
Thrift   238
Travel   239
Valentine's Day   241
Victory   241
Virtue   242
Wales   243
War   244
Wealth   244
Weddings   245
Wine and Spirits   257
Wisdom   262
Wives   264
Women   265
Work   269
Writers and Writing   270
Acknowledgments   271
Index   277

Introduction

Toasting is one of the easiest ways of marking special occasions, of turning an ordinary celebration into something extraordinary. Having been born and raised in the nation's capital, in a family of statesmen, politicians, and military leaders, I was introduced to toasting at a very early age. I remember my grandfather, Ambassador Joseph E. Davies, my uncle, Senator Millard Tydings and my father, General Burdette Fitch, giving toasts at family gatherings. They were all good speakers and I thought toasting a wonderful custom. Usually, once someone first makes a toast, others rise to the occasion. A good toast can make any gathering unique. It can be a few lines or even just a word or two, tender or bawdy, and on just about every conceivable subject.

It is good to remember, though, not to make your toast too long since people may get bored and stop paying attention. Because many diplomats tend to turn their toasts into policy statements, rambling on and on, the State Department's Office of Protocol now suggests that White House and diplomatic toasts be limited to no more than three minutes. Short and to the point is usually best, with the occasional exception. Toasting is a genteel civility designed to enhance an occasion. A bad toast can cast a pall over it.

Toasting is also almost always associated with alcoholic beverages, but that is a purely personal choice. There is a superstition that toasting with water brings bad luck, but juice, sodas, or any other liquid can be substituted. As a child I can remember toasting with milk.

Toasts can help us recall special moments. Who could ever forget Humphrey Bogart as Rick in *Casablanca* when he says, "Here's looking at you, kid"?

Perhaps wedding or anniversary toasts make you misty-eyed, or bachelor toasts make you laugh. Whatever the occasion, you will find it that much sweeter, funnier, and more memorable with the addition of a toast.

Wassail, the traditional British drink served in a large punch bowl or loving cup on Christmas and Twelfth Night, is derived from the Saxon term *waes hail*, meaning "to your health." Our modern custom of Christmas caroling from door to door came down from the time when people took the wassail bowl from neighbor to neighbor, expecting it to be replenished at every stop, while singing songs of the holiday season.

The expression *toast* or *toasting* dates back to the sixteenth or early-seventeenth century, although the custom is far older. The word *toast* comes to us from the Middle English *tosten* and the Middle French *toster*, which in turn was derived from Late Latin *tostare*, "to roast," and the past participle of *torrere*, "to dry, parch."

The name also derives from the medieval practice, begun by the French in the sixth century, of dropping a piece of spiced, toasted bread into a goblet of wine that was passed among the guests. Afterward, the piece of toast was given to the highest ranking lady or the most honored guest. The tradition of putting toast in the wine is still observed in the loving cups of some of the old universities.

Since poisoning was common in the Middle Ages, toasting provided a polite way of proving to the guests that the wine was safe to drink. Perhaps as additional proof, and certainly as a sign of friendship, the universal toast the world over became "to your health."

The practice of toasting can be traced back even further to many cultures in ancient times. It is probably the ancient Greeks and Romans we remember best. In both Greek and Roman mythology three portions of wine must be spilled on the ground and pledged to Mercury, the Graces, and Zeus before it is considered proper to drink. The Romans actually had an *"arbiter bibendi,"* or "toastmaster," at their banquets and dinners. He was literally "the judge of the drinking" since he kept an eye on the amount of wine consumed. He also judged the proportions of water to be mixed with the wine, since the wine served then was stronger than it is today. The Roman gladiators had their own rather macabre toast to Caesar before they went into the arena: *"Ave Caesar, morituri te salutamus,"* Latin for "Hail, Caesar, we who are about to die salute you."

In the early Christian era it was believed that the sound of the glasses being "clinked" during a toast would banish Satan from the premises. And the Vikings used human skulls as drinking goblets. We should all be thankful that modern Swedes long ago gave up the practice begun by their Viking forefathers. Their traditional toast, *skaal,* literally means "drinking vessel" and comes from the word skull. When Lord Byron heard about this custom he didn't rest until he acquired a skull goblet for himself.

In 1745, when Bonnie Prince Charlie was forced to flee Scotland following the Jacobite Rebellion, he sought exile in France. After that, whenever the Scottish regiments were forced to toast the English monarch, they would make sure their goblets passed over a vessel of water before toasting, thereby ensuring that they were really toasting "the King over the ocean," Bonnie Prince Charlie, rather than the English monarch.

I've heard some amusing anecdotes about famous individuals in toasting situations. In one story, George Bernard Shaw was put in a decidedly awkward position at a formal dinner. Following the English custom at the turn of the century, the host selected the topic of the toast as well as the guest who would give it. Trying to catch the literary lion at a loss for words, he assigned to Shaw the topic of "sex," a taboo subject in polite society. Without blinking an eye, Shaw toasted, "It is my great pleasure!"

My grandfather Davies told me another entertaining story about President Coolidge when my grandfather and grandmother attended a formal dinner at the White House. President Coolidge was known for being a man of few words; his nickname was "Silent Cal." The president's dinner partner that evening was a well-known Washington flirt. During the course of the meal she coyly batted her eyes at the president and said, "Mr. President, I have a one-hundred-dollar bet that

I can persuade you to give a toast of at least three words." That was a lot of money at the time, but "Silent Cal" lived up to his name. His immediate response was, "You lose!"

I have been asked for toasts on so many different occasions and in so many categories that I decided to write this book. If reading it makes you want to stand up and toast, then I shall have succeeded in my endeavor and be very pleased indeed! As a freelance photojournalist specializing in travel and yachting, I have collected these toasts throughout the world, on cruise ships, airplanes, trains, and even on safari. I've had a rollicking good time doing it and in the process my husband and I have met some amazing individuals and made some wonderful friends—which is what life is all about!

How to Use This Book

In most countries it is common to drink a toast to one's "health," but one can toast on any subject to suit a particular occasion, such as birthdays, holidays, the birth of a child, etc. No diplomatic occasion, state dinner, banquet, formal luncheon or dinner, wedding, anniversary, or christening would be complete without the ritual of toasting. Once I embarked upon this project, I wanted to write a comprehensive book of toasts for every occasion. I did not want to pad the book by listing the same toast in several categories, as others have done. For that reason, I included an index cross-referencing the toast to as many categories as applied. Because some toasts fit into at least two or even three or four categories, I encourage you to check the index and not just the Contents page to find every toast that applies to a particular category. Some toasts are similar in content but with a slightly different wording which gives them a completely different meaning.

I have tried to include only the best toasts, the easiest to remember, and a great many that have never been published before. I wanted them to be short and pithy and easy to follow. There are some notable exceptions, one of which is the literary toast written by David Martin, which was just too wonderful not to include. It's easy to tell that David Martin lives near our nation's capital. For maximum enjoyment, this toast should be read aloud so that you can appreciate the cadence. Those in the song category and a few others are a bit longer than the norm.

Although the vast majority of toasts are in English, there are quite a few in other languages, mostly Latin. The Romans were great toasters! The translations that follow are literal in most cases, except when it made more sense to translate them freely. To the best of my knowledge they are all spelled correctly with the proper accents. You may give them in their original language to impress the audience with your knowledge of languages or use the English translations. You will notice a few of my own toasts, which I have written over the years.

There is also a form on the last page of this book on which to send original toasts that you'd like me to include in future editions.

Just remember: If you are looking for something humorous, do not stop with the toasts in the humor section, but go to the index and see all the toasts that are cross-referenced to humor. I have tried not to include many sexist toasts, and have limited them to the Risqué and Humor categories.

For the most part *I* or *we* can be exchanged for *he* or *she*. I entered all toasts in the gender in which I received them.

If you are new to toasting, practice aloud with some of the shorter ones until you feel comfortable, and then advance to the longer ones. It is important to be as relaxed as possible when engaging in any form of public speaking, which is why practicing before the big event is a great help.

Following is a list of how "To your health" is said in different languages and countries around the world. In most cases these toasts were given to me by the various embassies. Following that I have tried to bring you toasts for every possible occasion. May you enjoy reading this book as much as I did researching and writing it. So "cheers," "cin cin," and "iechyd da!" Grab a cool drink and read on.

International—To Your Health

Afghanistan	Be salamati shoma
Albania	Gëzuar
Algeria	Fi se hetak
Angola	A sua felicidade
Arabian	Hanya, Bismillah
Armenia	Genatzt
Austria	Prosit
Bahrain	Besahtak
Belgium	Op uw gezonheid
Brazil	Saúde
Bulgaria	Nazdrave
Burma	Kyenmabazi
Canada	To your health, À vôtre santé
China	Kan bei, Nien nien nu e
Czech Republic	Na zdraví, Do dna (empty the glass)
Denmark	Skål
Dutch	Proost
Egypt	Fee sihetak
Eskimo	Chimo
Estonia	Tervist

Ethiopia	Letanachin
Finland	Kippis
France	À vôtre santé
Gaelic	Sheed arth (May you enjoy the good things in life)
Germany	Prost, zum Wohl
Great Britain	Your health, Cheers
Greece	Eis Igian, Stin ygia sou, Secgea, Stin iyia sas
Hawaiian	Kou ola Kino, Okole maluna, E kamau ki'aha kakou
Hungary	Kedves egeszsegere
Hebrew	L'chayim (To Life)
Iceland	Santanka nu
Ilokano	Agbiagtayo
India	Jaikind; Aanand
Indonesia	Selamat
Iran	Besalmati
Ireland	Seo do shláinte
Isle of Man	Shoh slaynt diu
Israel	L'chayim (To Life), Mazel tov (Congratulations)
Italy	Salute, A la Salute, Cin cin
Ivory Coast	Yako
Japan	Banzai, Kampai (Bottoms up)
Jordan	Besehtak
Korea	Kon gang ul wi ha yo
Kuwait	Besahatek, Sihitak
Liechtenstein	Auf ihre gesundheit

Lithuania	I sveikata
Luxembourg	Gesondhét
Macao	Tso' nei kinho
Malaysia	Slamat minum
Malta	Evviva
Mongolia	Tany eruul mendiin tuloo
Morocco	Sahtek
Nepal	Swasthya
Netherlands	Proost, Op uw gezondheid
New Zealand	Kia ora
Norway	Skål
Pakistan	Aap ki sehat hay liye, Sanda bashi
Philippines	Mabuhay
Poland	Na zdrowie, Vivat
Portugal	A sua saúde
Romania	Noroc
Russia	Na zdoróvie, Za vash zdorovia
Samoa	Ia Manuia (blessings)
Scotland	Sláinte
Spain	Salud
Sweden	Skål
Tagalog	Mabuhay (long life)
Tanzania	Kwa afya yako
Thailand	Sawasdi, Chaiyo (victory)
Turkey	Serefe
Ukrania	Boovatje zdorovi
Wales	Iechyd da
Yugoslavia	Ziveli, Zivio
Zulu	Oogy wawa

Similar Toasts from Different Nations

Below are a few toasts that although from different countries have virtually the same meaning.

Here's health and prosperity to your enemies' enemies.

• WELSH •

Here's a health to your enemies' enemies.

• IRISH •

Here's to us—
Few like us,
And none better!

• WELSH •

Here's tae us,
Wha's like us,
Damnt few and they're awe ded!
(Here's to us,
And those who are like us,
Damn few and they're all dead!)

• SCOTTISH •

Here's to us.
There are not many like us
And not many like us!

• OSCAR WILDE, CORRUPTION OF A CELTIC TOAST •

May the road you travel rise gently to meet you,
May the sun shine warmly on your face,
May the wind blow strongly on your back,
As the rain falls gently on the fields,
And may God hold you safely in his hands until we
meet again.

• SCOTTISH •

May the road rise to meet you,
May the wind be always at your back,
The sun shine warmly upon your face,
The rain fall soft upon your fields,
And until we meet again may God hold you in the
hollow of his hand.

• IRISH •

Slioc Sleacta
ar slioc do sleacta.
(A generation of a generation
to the generation of your generation.)

• IRISH •

May there be a generation of children
On the children of your children.

• CELTIC •

Toasts By Category

Absent Friends

Here's to absent friends,
And here's twice to absent enemies.

• IRISH •

Here's to absent friends,
Particularly to prosperity.

• CELTIC •

Here's to our absent friends,
In the hopes that wherever they are,
They're drinking to us.

Here's to our faraway friends,
May their spirits be with us,
As soon as these spirits are in us.

Here's to the girl that I love best,
I picked her out from all the rest,
She's not here to take her part,
So I'll drink to her with all my heart.

Oh, here's to other meetings,
And merry greetings then,
And here's to those we've drunk with,
But never can again.

• STEPHEN DECATUR •

To absent friends, though out of sight,
We recognize them with our glasses.

Accountants

Here's to my accountant,
He tells me what to do with my money,
After I've already spent it!

Here's to my accountant,
May he always make brilliant deductions!

Here's to my accountant,
If we had royalty in America,
He'd surely be "A Count"!

To accountants, the people who really
Know the score in business.

Action

Here's to doing and drinking,
Not sitting and thinking.

May we always have the class,
To rise up off our ass,
When there are deeds to be done
Or novel ways to have fun!

May we be judged by our actions,
Action is eloquence.

Actors

Here's to the Actor, friendliest of men!
Who "takes the part" of others now and then,
And if with a comrade he gets in a rage,
He's sure to "make up" ere he seeks the stage!

To the actor, a man who tries to be everything but
himself.

To the actor, a paradox who plays when he works,
And works when he plays.

Adolescence

To adolescence, that period
When children feel their parents
Should be told the facts of life.

To adolescence, that period
When children refuse to believe that someday
They'll be as dumb as their parents.

Adventure

A health to the man on the trail tonight,
May his dogs keep their legs,
May his matches never misfire.

• JACK LONDON •

Here's to you and here's to me,
Wherever we may roam,
And here's to the health and happiness
Of all the ones left at home.

Wealth I ask not, hope nor love,
Nor a friend to know me,
All I ask is the heav'n above,
And the roads below me!

● ROBERT LOUIS STEVENSON ●

Advertising

Here's to advertising,
Doing business without it is like winking at a girl in
the dark.
You know what you're doing, but nobody else does!

● STUART HENDERSON BRITT ●

Advice

Good, better, best,
Never let it rest,
Till your good is better,
And your better best!

Here are some good words to live by,
Love to one, friendship to many,
And good will to all!

Here's to the wisdom of all those
Who come to us seeking advice.

Age

Do not resist growing old,
Many are denied the privilege!

• IRISH •

God grant you many and happy years,
Till, when the last has crowned you,
The dawn of endless days appears,
And heaven is shining round you!

• OLIVER WENDELL HOLMES •

Grow old with me!
The best is yet to be,
The last of life,
For which, the first is made.

• ROBERT BROWNING •

Here's that we may live to eat the hen
That scratches on our grave.

• IRISH •

It is not the years in your life,
But the life in your years that counts.

• ADLAI STEVENSON •

May our lives, like the leaves of the maple,
Grow more beautiful as they fade,
May we say our farewells, when it's time to go,
All smiling and unafraid.

May the good Lord take a liking to you,
But not too soon!

May you live as long as you want,
And not want as long as you live.

May you live as long as you want,
And want to as long as you live!

May you die in bed at age ninety-five,
Shot by the jealous husband of a teenage wife.

• IRISH •

May the pleasures of youth
Never bring us pain in old age.

May the warmth of our affection
Survive the frosts of age.

May there be spring enough in your life
To outlast the winters.

May virtue and truth,
Guide you in youth,
Catnip and sage,
Cheer your old age.

• IRISH •

May we keep a little of the fuel of youth
To warm our body in old age.

Noah was six hundred years old before he knew how
to build an ark,
So don't lose your grip.

Sto lat niech zyje nam.
(One hundred years of life for us.)

• POLISH •

You're not as young as you used to be,
But you're not as old as you're going to be, so watch it!

• IRISH •

To age and treachery,
May they always overcome youth and skill.

To Age! To Age! Why does one care?
As the wrinkles grow longer and gray graces your
hair.
Life should be simple because when push comes to
shove,
The only one counting is the good Lord above!

To middle age, the time when a man is always
thinking
That in a week or so he'll feel as good as ever.

• DON MARQUIS •

To old age,
May it always be ten years older than I am!

To the metallic age!
Gold in our teeth,
Silver in our hair,
And lead in our pants!

To the old, long life and treasure;
To the young, all health and pleasure.

• BEN JONSON •

You're not too old when your hair turns gray,
You're not too old when your teeth decay.
But you'll know you're awaiting that final sleep,
When your mind makes promises your body can't
keep.

What is but age? Something to count?
Some people fight it as if climbing the mount.
I choose to live with dignity and grace,
And offer a drink to all in this place!

When there's snow on the roof,
There's fire in the furnace.

• CELTIC •

Agents

Here's to my agent,
Who never ever sells me short!

• Jennifer Rahel Conover •

Alimony

To alimony, giving comfort to the enemy.

To alimony, the high cost of loving!

To alimony, man's (woman's) best proof
That you have to pay for your mistakes.

To alimony, something that happens
When two people make a mistake,
And one of them has to keep on paying for it!

Ambition

Aut viam inveniam aut faciam.
(I will find a way or I shall make one.)

• LATIN •

Here's to great ambition,
About which people rant,
It makes you want to do things,
That everyone knows you can't!

America

America and England, may they never have any
division,
But the Atlantic between them.

• CHARLES DICKENS •

America, my country, great and free,
Heart of the world, I drink to thee.

Here's a toast to three great American birds:
May you always have an eagle in your pocket,
A chicken on your table,
And Wild Turkey in your glass.

Here's to America, the land of the push,
Where a bird in the hand is worth two in the bush,
But where every American, boy and man,
Knows a push in the bush
Is worth two in the hand.

Here's to the American eagle,
That bird so uncommonly hale,
Whom nobody yet could inveigle
When they tried to put salt on his tail.

One flag, one land, one heart,
One nation evermore.

• OLIVER WENDELL HOLMES •

To America, let us always remember,
The last two syllables of American
Are "I CAN"!

To her we drink, for her we pray,
Our voices silent never,
For her we'll fight come what may,
The Stars and Stripes forever.

To the land we love,
And the love we land.

To the United States, where each man is protected
by the Constitution,
Regardless of whether or not he has ever taken the
time to read it.

Anniversary

Here's to loving, to romance and to us,
May we travel together through time.
Alone we count as none, but together we're one,
For our partnership puts love to rhyme.

Here's to you both,
A perfect pair,
On the anniversary of your love affair.

Let anniversaries come and go,
But may your happiness go on forever.

To my spouse here's a health to the future,
A sigh for the past,
We can love and remember,
And love to the last.

To my spouse,
Because I love you truly,
Because you love me, too,
My very greatest happiness,
Is sharing life with you.

To you on your anniversary,
May every new day bring more happiness than
yesterday.

To your coming anniversaries,
May they be outnumbered
Only by your coming pleasures.

With fifty years between you
And your well-kept wedding vow,
The Golden Age, old friends of mine,
Is not a fable now.

• JOHN GREENLEAF WHITTIER •

Antiques

To antiques, I've (we've) gone from collecting them
To being one (of them)!

If I should live to a ripe old age,
May I possess some bit of charm, individuality and wit,
That I may not be discarded when I am withered,
worn and weak,
But sought after and cherished like a fine antique!

April Fools' Day

Let us toast the fools; but for them
The rest of us could not succeed.

• MARK TWAIN •

Architects

Here's to the ivy
That eventually covers our mistakes.

To the architect, one who drafts a plan of your house,
And plans a draft of your money.

• AMBROSE BIERCE •

Athletes

May we build muscles
Everywhere but in our heads.

To those whose bodies are temples,
May you never build an unwanted addition.

Attitude

Here's to attitude, which is contagious,
So make sure yours is worth catching!

Here's to attitude, such a small thing
That makes such a big difference!

If you turn your face toward the sun,
You will never see life's shadows.

• CELTIC •

Our lives are not determined by what happens to us,
But by how we handle it,
A positive attitude causes a chain reaction,
Which creates extraordinary results!

We become what we give ourselves
The power to be.

Babies

A baby will make love stronger, days shorter,
Nights longer, bankroll smaller, home happier,
Clothes shabbier, the past forgotten,
And the future worth living for.

A lovely being scarcely formed or moulded,
A rose with all its sweetest leaves yet folded.

• LORD BYRON •

Here's to one who born will be,
Born of the body, sowed of the soul,
Born of the flesh of you and me.

Here's to our grandchildren, gifts from on high,
It's God's way of compensating us for growing old!

• CELTIC •

Here's to the stork,
A most valuable bird,
That inhabits the residence districts.
He doesn't sing tunes,
Nor yield any plumes,
But he helps with the vital statistics!

I wish you happiness, I wish you joy,
I wish you first a little boy,
When his hair begins to curl,
I wish you then a little girl.

May your children always have
A rich father and a beautiful mother.

"The stork has brought a little peach!"
The nurse said with flair,
"I'm mighty glad," the father said,
"He didn't bring a pair."

To the new baby, who,
As the parents will soon find out,
Is the perfect example of minority rule.

To the new parents,
Who are about to enter a "changing" world!

To your newborn, An alimentary canal,
With a loud noise at one end,
And no responsibility at the other!

Bachelors and Bachelorettes

Drink, my buddies, drink with discerning,
Wedlock's a lane where there is no turning,
Never was owl more blind than lover,
Drink and be merry, lads, and think it over.

• BACHELOR PARTY TOAST •

Here's to the bachelorette,
She looks but will not leap.

'Tis better to have loved and lost,
Than to marry and be bossed.

To the bachelor,
A man who can have a girl on his knees,
Without having her on his hands.

To the bachelor,
A man who prefers to ball without the chain.

To the bachelor, that callous unthinking man
Who has cheated some poor worthy woman
Out of a divorce.

To the bachelorette,
A woman who won't take yes for an answer.

Bakers

May we never be done so much
As to make us crusty.

Baldness

To baldness, proof of the old adage,
Hair today and gone tomorrow!

To our bald friend,
Whose head is a shining example to us all!

Bankers

To our friend the banker,
May he never lose interest.

Beauty

Here's to a face that could stop a clock,
For she is so lovely and so fair,
That even time would linger there.

Beer and Ale

Champagne costs too much,
Whiskey's too rough,
Vodka puts big mouths in gear.
This little refrain
Should help to explain
Why it's better to order a beer!

In vino veritas
In cervesio felicitas.
(In wine there is wisdom, In beer there is joy.)

• LATIN •

For every wound, a balm.
For every sorrow, cheer.
For every storm, a calm.
For every thirst, a beer.

Here's a toast to the roast that good fellowship
lends,
With the sparkle of beer and wine;
May its sentiment always be deeper, my friends,
Than the foam at the top of the stein.

Here's to beer,
So much more than just a breakfast drink!

• SIGN IN A WELSH PUB •

Here's to a girl I love,
Would that she were nigh,
If drinking beer would bring her here,
I'd drink the damn place dry!

In heaven there is no beer,
So we'd better drink it here!

Let's drink the liquid of amber so bright,
Let's drink the liquid with foam snowy white,
Let's drink the liquid that brings all good cheer,
Oh, where is the drink like old-fashioned beer?

Man's way to God is with beer in hand.

• NIGERIA •

None so deaf as those who will not hear,
None so blind as those who will not see
But I'll wager none so deaf nor blind that he
Sees not nor hears me say come drink this beer.

• W. L. HASSOLDT •

Of all my favorite things to do,
The utmost is to have a brew.
My love grows for my foamy friend,
With each thirst-quenching elbow bend.
Beer's so frothy, smooth and cold,
It's paradise, pure liquid gold.
Yes, beer means many things to me,
But that's all for now, I gotta pee!

Pure water is the best gift a man can bring.
But who am I that I should have the best of anything?
Let princes revel at the pump, let peers with ponds
make free,
Beer is good enough for me.

• LORD NEAVES •

There once was a girl from Anheuser,
Who swore that no one could surprise her.
But Pabst took a chance,
Found the Schlitz in her pants,
And now she is sadder Budweiser.

You foam within our glasses, you lusty golden brew,
Whoever imbibes takes fire from you.
The young and the old sing your praises,
Here's to beer,
Here's to cheer,
Here's to beer!

• FROM THE OPERA *THE BARTERED BRIDE*,
BEDRICH SMETANA •

When money's tight and hard to get,
And your horse is an also-ran,
When all you have is a heap of debt
A pint of plain is your only man.

• IRISH •

Who'd care to be a bee and sip
Sweet honey from the flower's lip,
When he might be a fly and steer
Headfirst into a can of beer?

Best Wishes

May bad fortune follow you all your days,
And never catch up!

• IRISH •

May you be hung, drawn and quartered,
Hung in the hall of fame,
Drawn by a golden chariot,
And quartered in the arms of the one you love best.

May your well never run dry.

• IRISH •

Success to the lover, honor to the brave,
Health to the sick, and freedom to the slave.

Better Times

Ad astra per aspera.
(To the stars through difficulties.)

• LATIN •

To better times and a speedy calm to the storms of
life.

To better times,
For this has been a religious experience,
A living hell!

Come fill the bowl, each jolly soul;
Let Bacchus guide our revels;
Join cup to lip, with "hip, hip, hip,"
And bury those blue devils!

Here's to thee, my honest friend,
Wishing these hard times to mend.

Laugh and the world laughs with you;
Weep and it gives you the laugh anyway.

May the saints protect you,
And sorrow neglect you,
And bad luck to the one,
That doesn't respect you.

• Irish •

May the sunshine of comfort dispel the clouds of
despair.

May the sun shine upon you, lighting your way,
So that darkness may leave and perish today.

May you always see the island of opportunity
In the midst of every difficulty.

May you leave everything
A little better than when you found it.

Birthdays

Although another year has passed,
You look no older than the last!

Another candle on your cake?
Well, that's no cause to pout.
Be glad you have the strength
To blow the damn thing out!

Another year older? Just look at it this way:
You're only one day older than yesterday!

Happy birthday to you and many to be,
With friends that are true as you are to me!

Here's to you on your birthday,
Count the nights by stars, not shadows,
Count your life by smiles, not tears,
And with joy on every birthday,
Count your age by friends, not years.

Here's to you on your birthday,
It's better to be over the hill than under it!

Here's to you on your birthday,
No matter how old you are you don't look it!

I raise my glass to say,
It's your birthday, that's true,
And to celebrate the fact
That I'm younger than you!

Long may you live and may you die in your own
bed!

• CELTIC •

May you have been born under your lucky star,
And may that star never lose its twinkle.

May you live to be a hundred years
with one extra year to repent!

• IRISH •

May the best of the first (50) years,
Be the least of the next (50) years of your life!

Time marches on,
Now tell the truth,
Where did you find,
The fountain of youth?

To you on your birthday, glass held on high,
I'm glad it's you that's older and not I!

We wish you joy on your birthday
And all the whole year through,
For all the best that life can hold
Is none too good for you.

Blacksmiths

Here's a success to forgery.

Blessings

Always remember to forget
The troubles that passed away.
But never forget to remember
The blessings that come each day.

Bendith Duw for ar eich tai a phob fhyw rai o'ch dynion.
(The blessings of God on your house and on your
kith and kin.)

• WELSH •

Bless you and yours
As well as the cottage you live in.
May the roof overhead be well thatched
And those inside be well matched.

Do all the good you can,
By all the means you can,
In all the ways you can,
At all the times you can,
To all the people you can,
As long as ever you can.

• JOHN WESLEY •

For what we are about to receive,
May the Lord make us truly thankful.
Thank you, Lord, for what we've had,
But if we'd had a little bit more,
We'd have been right glad.

Four blessings upon you . . .
Older whiskey,
Younger women,
Faster horses,
And more money!

Get on your knees
And thank the Lord
You're on your feet.

God, Our Father, Be our strength when seas are
high,
Be our compass when we lose our way,
Be our anchor when we are adrift,
Be our beacon when we're in the dark,
Now bless us and the food we are about to receive
from your bountiful hands.

Good food,
Good meat,
Good God,
Let's eat!

May all be fed,
May all be healed,
May all be loved.

• JOHN ROBBINS •

May the blessings of each day
Be the blessings you need most.

May the blessings of light be upon you,
Light without and light within.
And in all your comings and goings,
May you ever have a kindly greeting,
From them you meet along the road.

May the Irish hills caress you.
May her lakes and rivers bless you.
May the luck of the Irish enfold you.
May the blessings of Saint Patrick behold you.

• IRISH •

May there always be work for your hands to do,
May your purse always hold a coin or two,
May the sun always shine on your windowpane,
May a rainbow be certain to follow each rain,
May the hand of a friend always be near to you,
May God fill your heart with gladness to cheer you.

• IRISH •

May you and yours live out your days
With happy hearts and peaceful ways,
May all your fondest dreams come true
With never a breath of sorrow and rue.
I bless you with this, three times three,
in love and plenty. So mote it be.

• MARIANNE WILLMAN IN *THE LOST BRIDE* •

May your neighbors respect you,
Trouble neglect you,
The angels protect you,
And heaven accept you.

May your troubles be less,
And your blessings be more,
And nothing but happiness come through your door.

• IRISH •

Bosses

To our boss,
The star to which we have all hitched our wagons.

To the boss,
The person who's early when you're late,
And late when you're early.

Builders

Drinks are on the house,
So someone get a ladder!

Here's to the carpenter,
He came, he sawed and he fixed it!

Here's to the man who comes home every day,
And says his work was riveting.

Celebration

Drink and be merry,
For our time on earth is short,
And death lasts forever.

Phagomen kai piomen, aurion gar thanoumetha.
(Let us eat and drink, for tomorrow we die.)

• EPICURUS OF SAMOS, GREEK •

Celebrities and Well-Known Individuals

A man is only as old as the woman he feels!

• GROUCHO MARX •

Drink is the feast of reason and the flow of soul.

• ALEXANDER POPE •

Forgive your enemies, but remember their names!

• JOHN F. KENNEDY •

Here's hoping that you live forever
And mine is the last voice you hear!

• WILLARD SCOTT •

Here's looking at you, kid!

• HUMPHREY BOGART IN *CASABLANCA* •

Here's to the contemptible scoundrel that stole the cork from my lunch.

• W. C. FIELDS •

I drink no more than a sponge.

• FRANÇOIS RABELAIS •

I have taken more out of alcohol than alcohol has taken out of me.

• WINSTON CHURCHILL •

I'm like old wine: They don't bring me out very often, but I'm well preserved.

In matters of style,
Swim with the currents.
In matters of principle,
Stand like a rock.

It's still the same old story,
A fight for love and glory,
A case of do or die!
The world will always welcome lovers
As time goes by.

Live long and prosper!

May the force be with you!

May the groom's heart be filled with hope,
And the bride's shoes be filled with lead!

• WEDDING TOAST IN THE 1999 FILM *RUNAWAY BRIDE* •

Moderation is a fatal thing, nothing succeeds like
excess.

• OSCAR WILDE •

Never go to bed mad.
Stay up and fight!

• PHYLLIS DILLER •

There comes a time in every woman's life,
When the only thing that helps is a glass of
champagne.

• BETTE DAVIS •

To sight, sound, touch,
To work, to laugh,
And most of all to prevail!

• LAUREN BACALL •

To the confounding of our enemies!

• DEAN ACHESON, A CORRUPTION OF A CELTIC TOAST •

To the most distinguished group of people to grace
this room
Since Thomas Jefferson dined alone.

• JOHN F. KENNEDY TO A GROUP OF NOBEL PRIZE
WINNERS AT THE WHITE HOUSE •

The meeting of two personalities is like the contact
of two chemical substances;
If there is any reaction, both are transformed.

• CARL JUNG •

To women, wild and wonderful,
May they be the last things to be subjugated by man!

• HAL HOLBROOK ON THE TV SERIES
DESIGNING WOMEN •

Two roads diverged in a wood, and I
I took the one less traveled by,
And that has made all the difference.

• ROBERT FROST •

Wherever I roam, whatever realms I see,
My heart untravelled fondly turns to thee.

• OLIVER GOLDSMITH •

Work is the curse of the drinking class.

• OSCAR WILDE •

Challenges

Small minds are cowed by misfortune,
But great minds rise above it.

Champagne

Here's champagne to our real friends,
And real pain to our sham friends.

Here's to champagne, that drink divine,
It makes us forget all our troubles.
It's made from a dollar's worth of wine
And five dollars' worth of bubbles.

Here's to roast beef when you're hungry,
Champagne when you're dry,
A lover when you need one,
And heaven when you die.

Here's to you with a glass full of bubbles,
To blow away all of your troubles.

Some take their gold in minted mold,
And some in harps hereafter,
But give me mine in bubbles fine
And keep the change in laughter.

• OLIVER HERFORD •

The bubble winked at me and said,
"You'll miss me, brother, when you're dead."

• OLIVER HERFORD •

The miser may be pleased with gold,
The ladies' man with a pretty lass,
But I'm best pleased when I behold,
This nectar sparkling in the glass.

Three be the things I shall never attain,
Envy, content, and sufficient champagne!

• DOROTHY PARKER •

To champagne, the drink that makes you see double
And feel single!

To the glorious, golden vintage of France,
Whose bubbling beauty our spirits entrance,
When with friends tried and true this nectar we quaff,
We wish for a neck like a thirsty giraffe.

Children

Here's to children,
The truest legacy we leave the world.

Mothers [fathers] hold their children's hands for
just a little while,
And their hearts forever.

In raising your children spend half as much money,
And twice as much time.

To our grandchildren,
Our revenge on our children!

• CELTIC •

There are only two lasting bequests we can hope to
give our children.
One of these is roots, the other wings.

• HODDING CARTER •

Chimney Sweeps

May you have a bright future,
The chimney sweep said to his son!

Christening

May God bless this precious baby on this her (his)
christening day.
May God's love and wisdom guide her (him) along
life's way.

May God bless you, Baby, on this special
christening day,
May He give you divine protection and guidance
in His loving way.

May this be the last bath at which your baby cries.

Christmas

A Christmas wish,
May you never forget what is worth remembering,
Or remember what is best forgotten.

• CELTIC •

A Merry Christmas this December
To a lot of folks I don't remember!

• FRANKLIN ADAMS •

At Christmas play and make good cheer,
For Christmas comes but once a year.

• THOMAS TUSSER •

Be merry all, be merry all,
With holly dress the festive hall,
Prepare the song, the feast, the ball,
To welcome Merry Christmas.

Blessed is the season, which engages the whole world
In a conspiracy of love!

• HAMILTON WRIGHT MABIE •

Cheers to Santa and cheers to you,
What "deers" you've been the whole year through.
We raise our glasses in cheers to say,
Antlers off to you in every way,
Merry Christmas and Happy New Year!

Christmas, a day when cheer and gladness blend,
When heart meets heart,
And friend meets friend.

• J. H. FAIRWEATHER •

Here's to friends we've yet to meet,
Here's to those here, all here I greet,
Here's to childhood, youth, old age,
Here's to prophet, bard and sage,
Here's to your health, may all be bright
On this so special Christmas night.

Here's to the day of good will,
Cold weather, and warm hearts.

Here's to the holly with its bright red berry,
Here's to Christmas, let's make it merry.

Here's to the white of the mistletoe,
And to its many leaves so green,
And here's to the lips of ruby red,
Waiting 'neath to complete the scene.

Here's to us all!
God bless us every one!

• Tiny Tim's toast, *A Christmas Carol*
by Charles Dickens •

Here's wishing you more happiness,
Than words can ever tell,
Not just for Christmas,
But all year round as well.

Holly and ivy all hung up,
And something wet in every cup!

• IRISH •

I know I've wished you this before,
But every year I wish it more,
Merry Christmas!

I wish you a Merry Christmas,
And a Happy New Year,
A pocket full of money,
And a cellar full of beer.

May peace and plenty be the first to lift the latch on
your door,
And happiness be guided to your home by the
candle of Christmas.

• CELTIC •

May you be poor in misfortune this Christmas
And rich in blessings,
Slow to make enemies,
Quick to make friends,
And rich or poor, slow or quick,
As happy as the New Year is long.

May you live as long as you wish,
And have all you wish as long as you live.
This is my Christmas wish for you.

May you never be without a drop at Christmas.

• IRISH •

May your corn stand high as yourself,
Your fields grow bigger with rain,
And the mare know her own way home on
Christmas night.

• IRISH •

May your sheep all have lambs,
But not on Christmas night.

• IRISH •

May yours be the first home in the parish
To welcome St. Nicholas

• IRISH •

Now, thrice welcome, Christmas!
Which brings us much good cheer,
Mince pies and plum pudding,
Strong ale and strong beer!

Clans

Here's to cousins, kissing and otherwise.

To our clan, the best there are,
Every woman, every man.

To my cousins,
Who always make it seem that everything is relative.

To my cousins overseas,
Blood is always thicker than water.

Coaches

Here's to our coach, a man who's willing to lay down
our lives
For his school.

Let's drink to the coach,
And hope he doesn't catch us.

To the man for whom sweat is sweet.

Congratulations

Congratulations, all our dreams can come true,
If we but have the strength and tenacity to
pursue them.

Congratulations, the strength of the team is in
each member,
And the strength of each member is in the team.

Congratulations, when you expect nothing
but the best,
You very often get it.

Courage

Courage does not always roar like a lion,
Sometimes it is a quiet voice at the end of the day
That says, "I will try again tomorrow."

Here's to you from morning till night,
Here's to the person with courage to fight,
The courage to fight and the courage to live,
The courage to learn, and to love, and forgive.

May the noise never excite us to battle,
Or confusion reduce us to defeat.

To courage, what lies behind and before us is
unimportant
Compared to what lies within us.

Creativity

What may seem today to be only a ripple,
Can be the wave of the future tomorrow.

Creditors

Here's to our creditors,
May they be endowed with the three virtues,
Faith, hope and charity.

Here's to the creditor,
Long may he waive.

Critics

To the critic,
Someone who likes to write,
About things he doesn't like.

Curses

Each must drain his cup of wine,
And I the first will toss off mine,
Thus I advise, here then I bid you all Wassail,
Cursed be he who will not say Drink Hail!

Here's to short shoes and long corns for our enemies.

May a band of gypsies camp in your belly,
And trained bears to dance on your liver.

May his cradle ne'er rock, may his box have no lock,
May his wife have no frock for to cover her back,
May his cock never crow, may his bellows ne'er blow,
And his pipe and his pot, may he ever more lack.

• IRISH •

May his pig never grunt, may his cat never hunt,
That a ghost may catch him in the dark of the night,
May his hen never lay, may his ass never bray,
And his goat fly away like an old paper kite.

• IRISH •

May she marry a ghost, and bear him a kitten,
And may the High King of glory permit it to get the
mange.

• IRISH •

May the devil make a ladder of our enemy's
backbone,
While he is picking apples in the garden of hell.

May the greatest doctors in the world
Know of your case.

May you be the proof that a human being can
endure anything.

May your sex life be as good as your credit.

Death and the Departed

A toast to your coffin,
May it be made of one hundred-year-old oak.
And may we plant the tree together, tomorrow.

• CELTIC •

Art is long, and Time is fleeting,
And our hearts, though stout and brave,
Still, like muffled drums, are beating
Funeral marches to the grave.

• HENRY WADSWORTH LONGFELLOW •

De mortuis nihil nisi bonum.
(Speak kindly of the dead.)

• LATIN TOAST TO THE DECEASED •

Here's to the tears of affection,
May they crystallize as they fall,
And become pearls, that in the after years
We'll wear in memory of those whom we have loved.

Ho, stand to your glasses, steady!
'Tis all we have left to prize.
A cup to the dead already,
Hurrah for the next that dies!

• BARTHOLOMEW DOWLING •

Let us make our glasses kiss,
Let us quench the sorrow-cinders.

• RALPH WALDO EMERSON •

May every hair on your head turn into a candle and
light your way to heaven,
And may God and the Holy Mother take the harm
of the years away from you.

• IRISH •

May you be in heaven,
A half hour before the Devil knows you're dead!

• IRISH •

May we all come to peaceful ends,
And leave our debts to our friends.

• IRISH •

Now let us sit and drink and make us merry,
And afterward we will his body bury.

• GEOFFREY CHAUCER •

Sit tibi terra levis.
(May the earth be light upon you.)

• LATIN •

Terra es, terram ibis.
(Dust thou art, to dust thou shalt return.)

• LATIN •

The good die young,
Here's hoping you live to a ripe old age!

• IRISH •

'Tis my will when I die, not a tear shall be shed,
No *"Hic Jacet"* be graved on my stone,
But pour o'er my coffin a bottle of red,
And write that "His Drinking is Done."

To live in the hearts we leave behind is not to die.

Wash me when dead in the juice of the vine,
dear friends!
Let your funeral service be drinking and wine,
dear friends!
And if you would meet again when the
Doomsday comes,
Search the dust of the tavern, and sift from it mine,
dear friends!
We toast his roguish and venerable shade.

• JAMES J. KILPATRICK'S TOAST TO H. L. MENCKEN ON
THE ONE HUNDRED FIRST ANNIVERSARY OF
MENCKEN'S BIRTH •

When you were born, you cried and the
world rejoiced,
Live your life so that when you die, the world cries
and you rejoice.

Defeat

Here's to the men who lose.
It is the vanquished's praises that I sing,
And this is the toast I choose,
A hard-fought failure is a noble thing!

It is better to fail with honor
Than to win with deceit.

It's better to lose on your own terms,
Than win on someone else's.

There are some defeats more triumphant than
victories,
This was one of them, so here's to us!

To our defeat, for,
If experience is the best teacher,
We are now truly educated.

To us, because any direction we go from here is up!

Victis honor.
(Let's hear it for the losers; or, honor to the
vanquished.)

• Latin •

Dentists

Here's to my dentist, who deals with the tooth,
The whole tooth and nothing but the tooth!

Here's to the dentist who got most of his training in
the military,
As a drill sergeant!

To the dentist, the person who runs a filling station,
And is a collector of old magazines.

To the dentist, who makes his living hand to mouth.

Diplomats

A statesman is an easy man, he tells his lies by rote.
A journalist invents his lies, and rams them down
your throat.
So stay at home and drink your beer and let the
neighbors vote!

• WILLIAM BUTLER YEATS •

A toast to any gentleman,
So shrewd and diplomatic,
Who never, though he's in his cups,
Decides he's operatic.

Here's to the diplomat,
Whose specialty is letting you have her (his) way.

To the diplomat, a person who can tell a man to go
to hell
In such a way that he'll look forward to making
the trip!

To the diplomat,
A person who is held upright
By equal pressure from all directions.

To the diplomat,
A person who has learned that you can't bend a nail
By hitting it squarely on the head.

To the diplomat, an ex-politician
Who has mastered the art of holding his tongue.

To the diplomat and diplomacy,
Which Ambrose Bierce defined as
The patriotic art of lying for one's country.

Discretion

A toast to the groom,
And discretion to his bachelor friends.

I have never been hurt
By anything I didn't say.

• CALVIN COOLIDGE •

With some folks,
It's what you don't say that counts.

Divorce

Here's to love,
Ain't love grand,
I just got a divorce from my old man,
And I did laugh at the judge's decision,
He gave the kids to Pop,
And they weren't even his'n!

Doctors and Medicine

Here's to good doctors,
They add life to your years,
Rather than years to your life!

Here's to Medicine, the only profession that labors
incessantly
To destroy the reason for its own existence.

If the patient dies, the doctor has killed him,
But if he gets well, the saints have saved him!

Dreams

Reach high, for the stars lie hidden in your soul,
Dream deep, for every dream precedes the goal.

Drink

A drink, my lass, in a deep clear glass,
    Just properly tempered by ice,
And here's to the lips mine have kissed,
    And if they were thine, here's twice.

And fill them high with generous juice,
    As generous as your mind,
And pledge me in the generous toast,
    The whole of humankind!

• ROBERT BURNS •

Come fill a flowing bowl until it does run over,
   Tonight we will all merry be,
   Tomorrow we'll get sober.

• JOHN FLETCHER •

Drink a bottle to us in London,
   And a stein in old Berlin,
   Some rare champagne,
   If you get to Spain,
   Is nice to remember us in;
You may drink to our health in Paris,
   With a flagon of old Cognac,
   But if you want the toast,
   That'll please us the most,
   Just bring us a bottle back.

Drink and be merry, for our time on earth is short,
   And death lasts forever.

• AMPHIS •

Drink and dance and laugh and lie,
   Love the reeling midnight through,
For tomorrow we will die, but alas we never do!

• DOROTHY PARKER •

Drink no longer water,
But use a little wine,
For thy stomach's sake,
And thine other infirmities.

• PLAQUE AT STONE HOUSE, KIRIKIRI, NEW ZEALAND •

Drink not to my past, which is weak and indefensible,
Nor to my present, which is not above reproach,
But let us drink to our futures, which thank
God are immaculate!

Drink to the girls and drink to their mothers,
Drink to their fathers and drink to their brothers;
Toast their dear healths as long as you are able,
And dream of their charms while you're
under the table!

Drink today and drown all sorrow,
You shall perhaps not do't tomorrow,
Best while you have it, use your breath,
There is no drinking after death.

• FRANCIS BEAUMONT AND JOHN FLETCHER •

Drink with impunity,
Or anyone who happens to invite you!

• ARTEMUS WARD •

Fill up the goblet, let it swim
In foam, that overlooks the brim,
He that drinks deepest, here's to him.

• CHARLES COTTON •

God made man as frail as a bubble,
God made love, and love made trouble,
God made wine and is it any sin,
For man to drink wine to drown the trouble in?

He who goes to bed, and goes to bed sober,
Falls as the leaves do, and dies in October;
But he who goes to bed, and does so mellow,
Lives as he ought to and dies a good fellow.

Here's to you and here's to me,
But as you're not here, here's two to me!

How beautiful the water is!
To me 'tis wondrous sweet,
For bathing purposes and such,
But liquor's better neat.

• MRS. C. O. SMITH •

I drink it as the Fates ordain it,
Come, fill it, and have done with rhymes,
Fill up the lonely glass, and drain it,
In memory of dear old times.

• WILLIAM MAKEPEACE THACKERAY •

I drink to your charm, your beauty, and your brains,
Which gives you a rough idea of how hard up I am
for a drink.

• GROUCHO MARX •

I drink to the health of another,
And the other I drink to is he,
In the hope that he drinks to another,
And the other he drinks to is me!

I prefer a well-known drinker,
To an anonymous alcoholic.

I thank you for your welcome, which was most cordial,
And for your cordial, which is most welcome!

If all be true as we do think,
There are five reasons why we drink,
Good wine, a friend, or being dry,
Or lest one should be, by and by,
Or any other reason why!

• HENRY ALDRICH •

May we never want a friend to cheer us,
Or a bottle to cheer him!

Nunc est bibendum!
(Now it's time to drink!)

• HORACE, LATIN •

Oh whiskey, rye whiskey,
I'll drink it 'til I die,
If the ocean were whiskey,
And I were a duck,
I'd dive to the bottom and drink my way up!

Plus je bois, mieux je chante!
(The more I drink, the better I sing!)

• FRENCH •

Ship me somewhere east of Suez,
Where the best is like the worst,
Where there aren't no Ten Commandments,
an' a man can raise a thirst.

• RUDYARD KIPLING •

The sun is always over the yardarm somewhere
over the world,
So drink!

Then fill the cup, fill high! fill high!
Nor spare the rosy wine.
If death be in the cup, we'll die,
Such death would be divine.

• JAMES RUSSELL LOWELL •

Then here's to the heartening wassail,
　　Wherever good fellows are found;
　　Be its master instead of its vassal,
　　And order the glasses around.

• OGDEN NASH •

There are many good reasons for drinking,
　　One has just entered my head,
　　If a man doesn't drink when he's living,
How the hell can he drink when he's dead?

• IRISH •

Thirsty days hath September,
　　April, June and November;
　　All the rest are thirsty too,
Except for him who hath home brew.

You shall and you shan't,
　　You will and you won't,
　　You're condemned if you do,
And you're damned if you don't,
　　So let's drink!

We'll drink the wanting into wealth,
And those that languish into health,
The afflicted into joy, the oppressed
Into serenity and rest.

• CHARLES COTTON •

Were't the last drop in the well,
As I gasp'd upon the brink,
Ere my fainting spirit fell,
'Tis to thee I would drink.

• LORD BYRON •

Drunkenness

Here's to the ten stages of drunkenness:
1. witty and charming
2. rich and famous
3. benevolent
4. clairvoyant
5. screw dinner
6. patriotic
7. crank up the *Enola Gay*
8. witty and charming, part II
9. invisible, and lastly
10. bulletproof

Not drunk is he who from the floor,
Can rise again and drink some more.
But drunk is he who prostrate lies,
And who can neither drink nor rise!

The only difference between an Irish wedding
And an Irish wake, is one less drunk.

• IRISH •

There is the love of a beautiful maiden,
There is the love of a very strong man,
There is the love of a babe who is unafraid,
There is the love of a man for his land,
But the most beautiful love is
The love that loves even stronger than that
of a mother,
It is the infinite constant brotherly love of one old
drunk for another!

When we drink, we get drunk.
When we get drunk, we fall asleep.
When we fall asleep, we commit no sin.
When we commit no sin, we go to heaven.
So, let's all get drunk, and go to heaven!

• IRISH •

Editors

Here's to my editor,
Who can read me like a book!

• JENNIFER RAHEL CONOVER •

Enemies

May the enemies of Wales (Ireland, Scotland)
Never meet a friend!

• WELSH •

May those who deceive us always be deceived!

May those who love us, love us,
And those that don't love us,
May God turn their hearts,
And if He doesn't turn their hearts,
May He turn their ankles,
So we'll know them by their limping.

• CELTIC •

May we treat our friends with kindness,
And our enemies with generosity.

Entrepreneurs

Here's to the entrepreneur,
Who knows that money doesn't talk nowadays,
It goes without saying.

Eternity

Here's to eternity,
May we spend it in as good company as this night
finds us.

Excellence

To excellence, which means caring more than some
think is wise,
Risking more than some think is safe,
Dreaming more than some think is sensible,
And working more than most are willing to do!

Family

Here's to the sap in the family tree!

Here's to your health, and your family's good health,
May you live long and prosper.

Here's to family,
A harbor of safety in an ocean of change.

Farewells

Friendly may we part and quickly meet again.

May we always part with regret,
And meet again with pleasure.

Merry met, and merry part,
I drink to thee with all my heart.

To farewells, may they be never spoken,
To friendships, may they never be broken.

Farmers

God speed the plough,
But keep me from the handles!

• YORKSHIRE •

Here's to fertility, the toast of agriculture,
And the bane of love.

May the frost never afflict your spuds,
May the outside leaves of your cabbage always be
free from worms,
May the crows never pick your haystack,
And may your donkey always be in foal.

May you always be able to distinguish
Between the weeds and the flowers.

O gie me the lass that has acres o' charm,
O gie me the lass wi' a well-stockit farm.

• SCOTTISH •

Fathers

My father has given me the greatest treasure a father
can give,
A piece of himself.

To my father, if I can become half the man he is,
I'll have achieved greatness.

Firemen

To firemen, may they never be "toasted,"
Save by the glass of their friends.

Fishing

Here's to fishing, a grand delusion,
Enthusiastically promoted by glorious liars in
old clothes!

• DON MARQUIS •

Here's to our favorite fisherman,
May he live long enough to hear his stories come true.

Here's to our fisherman bold,
Here's to the fish he caught,
Here's to the one that got away,
And here's to the ones he bought.

Here's to rod and line,
May they never part company.

Here's to the noble sport of fishing,
A hobby that we're all hooked on!

Here's to the steady fisherman,
Who never reels home!

Let's lift our glass to the creative fisherman,
Every time he talks about the one that got away it
grows another foot.

Lord, suffer me to catch a fish so large
That even I in talking of it afterward
Shall have no need to lie!

May good things come to those who bait.

May the holes in your net be no bigger than your
fish.

• IRISH •

To fishing, if it interferes with business,
Give up the business.

To old fishermen who never die,
They just smell that way!

To the fish, a creature that goes on vacation
About the same time most fishermen do.

To the fish who may come and go,
But the memory of afternoons on the stream
endures.

Focus

Here's to focus and determination,
Because obstacles are only those frightening things
you see
When you fail to focus on your goals.

Food

Eat, drink, and be merry, for tomorrow you diet.

Eat thy bread with joy,
And drink thy wine with a merry heart.

• ECCLESIASTES 9:7 •

Happiness being a dessert so sweet,
May life give you more than you can ever eat.

Only Irish coffee provides in a single glass,
All four essential food groups,
Alcohol, caffeine, sugar and fat!

To the alchemy that turns groceries into meals.

To the soup,
May it be seen and not heard.

Fourth of July

Here's to the Fourth of July,
For like oyster soup,
It can't be enjoyed without crackers.

Freedom •

Love, life, and liberty,
Love pure, live long, and liberty without end.

Friendship

A health to our friends and our wives,
May fortune smile on them the rest of their lives.

A little health, a little wealth,
A little house and freedom,
With some few friends for certain ends,
But little cause to need 'em.

A real friend is one who walks in
When the rest of the world walks out.

• WALTER WINCHELL •

A toast to the three things that are important
in this world,
Good health, peace with one's neighbor,
And friendship with all.

A true friend is the greatest of all blessings.

• Duc de la Rochefoucauld •

Always remember to forget the friends that
proved untrue,
But never forget to remember those that stuck by you!

Bread to feed our friendship,
Salt to keep it true,
Water is for a welcome,
And wine to drink with you.

• French •

Don't walk in front of me, I may not follow.
Don't walk behind me, I may not lead,
Just walk beside me and be my friend.

• Irish •

Forsake not an old friend, for the new is not
comparable to him.
A new friend is as new wine,
When it is old, thou shalt drink it with pleasure.

• ECCLESIASTES 9:10 •

Friends we are today,
And friends we'll always be,
For I am wise to you,
And you can see through me.

Friendship improves happiness, and abates misery,
By doubling our joy, and dividing our grief.

• JOSEPH ADDISON •

Friendship is the wine of life,
Let's drink of it and to it!

Good friends, good food, good times!

Here's to cold nights, warm friends,
And a good drink to give them.

Here's to friends,
They know you well,
But like you just the same!

Here's to friends,
Who hear the songs in my heart,
And sing them back to me,
When my memory fades.

Here's to friendship,
One soul in two bodies!

Here's to friendship, which is like the ocean,
Endless and deep.

Here's to one sweetheart, one bottle and one friend,
The first beautiful, the second full, and the last
forever faithful.

Here's to our best friends,
Who know the worst about us,
But still refuse to believe it!

Here's to our friends and the strength to put up
with them!

• AD FOR THE MOVIE *THE FOUR SEASONS* •

Here's to our friends as long as we're able,
To lift our glasses from the table.

Here's to the friends
Who listen to my advice, rejoice in my success,
Scorn my enemies, laugh at my jokes,
And ignore my ignorance.

Here's to the friends who love us well,
May the rest go straight to hell.

Here's to the key for unlocking friendship,
"Whis—key"!

Here's to us that are here, to you that are there,
and the rest of us everywhere!

• RUDYARD KIPLING •

If you want to enjoy an hour, make love,
If you want to enjoy a day, go fishing,
If you want to enjoy a year, get married,
If you want to enjoy a lifetime, make friends!

Keep the grasp of fellowship,
Which warms us more than wine.

• JULIA WARD HOWE •

Love to one, friendship to a few,
And good will to all.

May fortune still be kind to you,
And happiness be true to you,
And life be long and good to you,
Is the toast of all your friends to you.

• IRISH •

May friendship, like wine, improve as time advances,
And may we always have old wine, old friends, and
young cares

May good fortune precede you,
May love walk with you,
May good friends follow you.

• CELTIC •

May our injuries be written in sand,
And our friendships in stone.

May the barque of friendship never founder
On the rock of deceit.

May the hinges of friendship never rust,
Nor the wings of love lose a feather.

May we ever be able to serve a friend,
And noble enough to conceal it.

• CELTIC •

May we have a few real friends,
Rather than a thousand acquaintances.

• IRISH •

May we have more and more friends,
And need them less and less.

May we never have friends who, like shadows,
Keep close to us in the sunshine, only to desert us on
a cloudy day.

May we never want for a friend,
Nor a glass to give him!

• CELTIC •

May you always come more than you go.

May you have warm words on a cold evening,
A full moon on a dark night,
And the road downhill all the way to your door.

• IRISH •

May you never lie, steal, cheat or drink,
But if you must lie, lie in each other's arms,
If you must steal, steal kisses,
If you must cheat, cheat death,
And if you must drink, drink with us, your friends.

May your life be long and happy,
Your cares and sorrows few,
And the many friends around you,
Prove faithful, fond and true.

May your right hand always be stretched out in
friendship,
But never in want.

• IRISH •

Now I, friend, drink to you, friend,
As my friend drank to me,
And I, friend, charge you, friend,
As my friend charged me,
That you, friend, drink to your friend,
As my friend drank to me,
And the more we drink together, friend,
The merrier we'll be!

• IRISH •

Old friends are scarce,
New friends are few,
Here's hoping I've found
One of each in you.

Please save your cards and flowers,
We've drunk to your health so much,
We've almost ruined ours!

• (TO A SICK FRIEND) •

The Lord gives us relatives,
Thank God we can choose our friends!

The world is happy and colorful,
And life itself is new,
And I am very grateful for
The friend I found in you.

Then here's to thee, old friend, and long
May thou and I thus meet,
To brighten still with wine and song
This short life ere it fleet.

There is no possession more valuable than
A true and faithful friend.

• SOCRATES •

Through life's road with all its curves and bends,
Naught cheers the heart like old-time friends.

'Tis better to buy a small bouquet,
And give it to your friend this very day,
Than a bushel of roses white and red,
To lay on his coffin after he's dead.

To friendship, may differences of opinion cement it.

To old times, old friends, the best of friends.
To new times, new friends, the best of friends!

While wine and friendship crown the board,
We'll sing the joys that both afford.

• JOHN DYER •

Who is a friend but someone to toast,
Someone to jibe and someone to roast,
My friends are the best friends,
Loyal, willing and able,
Now let's get to drinking,
Glasses off the table!

Future

Here's to our future, the best way to predict it
Is to create it!

Gambling

Here's to poker, which is like a glass of beer,
You have to draw to fill it.

Brindo por tí, aunque mal pagues.
(I drink to you even though you reciprocate badly.)

• SPANISH, FROM COLOMBIA •

Call frequently, drink moderately,
Part friendly,
Pay today and trust tomorrow.

Cave quid dicis, quando, et cui!
(Be careful what you say, when and to whom!)

• LATIN •

Céad Míle Fáilte!
(A hundred million welcomes!)

• IRISH •

Como dijo el Padre Hidalgo, insultado el que deje algo.
(As Padre Hidalgo said, he who leaves anything [in his glass] is insulting.)

• MEXICAN •

Cool breeze. Warm fire.
Full moon. Easy chair.
Empty plates. Soft words.
Sweet songs. Tall tales.
Short sips. Long life.

• JOHN EGERTON •

Cymru Am Byth!
(Wales Forever!)

• WELSH •

Days of ease,
And nights of pleasure.

Dummheit frisst, intelligenz säuft!
(Stupid people eat, intelligent people drink!)

• GERMAN •

Ein little drink in the morning time is better
Als den ganzen dag gor kein!
(A little drink in the morning is better
Than the whole day none at all!)

• GERMAN/AMERICAN DIALECT •

Gaudeamus igitur juvenes dum sumus.
Post iucundum iuventutes,
Post molestam senectutem,
Nos habebit humus.
(So let us rejoice while we are young.
After happy youth,
After annoying old age,
The earth will have us.)

• LATIN •

Gentlemen, The Queen!

• CANADIAN •

Good day, good health,
Good cheer, good night!

Here's my top to your bottom,
And your bottom to my top,
May they meet in the middle.

Here's that we may always have
A clean shirt,
A clean conscience,
And a punt in our pocket.

• IRISH •

Here's to becoming top banana
Without losing touch with the bunch!

Here's to living well,
'Tis the best revenge!

Here's to the present,
The hell with the past!
A health to the future and joy to the last!

Here's to you and here's to me,
And here's to the girl with the dimpled knee,
And here's to the guy that unfastened her garter,
It wasn't much, but it was a damn good starter!

Here's to you and yours and to mine and ours,
And if mine and ours ever come across you and yours,
I hope you and yours will do as much for mine
and ours,
As mine and ours have done for you and yours!

• IRISH •

Here's to you, as good as you are,
And here's to me, as bad as I am,
But as good as you are and as bad as I am,
I am as good as you are, as bad as I am!

Here's to you,
Here's two to you,
And two to you two, too,
And to you two, too, here's two!

Here's to you, my dear,
And here's to the dear who's not here,
Because if that dear were here, my dear,
I wouldn't be drinking to you, my dear!

I raise my glass to wish you your heart's desire!

• RUSSIAN •

I'm as dear to you as he,
He's as dear to me as thee,
You're as dear to him as me,
Here's to three's good company.

Lang may your lum reek.
(Long may your chimney smoke; or, may you always
have fuel for your fire.)

• SCOTTISH •

Licor bendito, dulce tormento
Què haces afuera, vamos pa' dentro!
(Blessed liquor, that sweet torment
That you make outside and we take inside us!)

• SPANISH, FROM THE DOMINICAN REPUBLIC •

May our pleasures be forever free
From the stings of remorse!

May you always have walls for the wind,
A roof for the rain,
Drinks beside the fire,
Laughter to cheer you,
Those you love near you,
And all that your hearts might desire.

May your coffee and any slanders against you
Always be just alike—without grounds.

May the happiest days of your past
Be the saddest days of your future.

May the rest of your life be the best of your life!

May you live to learn well,
And learn to live well.

May you taste the sweetest pleasures
That fortune e'er bestowed,
And may all your friends remember
All the favors you are owed.

May we always look forward with pleasure,
And backward with regret!

• WELSH •

May we always think what we say,
Rather than say what we think.

May you have the hindsight to know where
you've been,
The foresight to know where you're going,
And the insight to know when you're going too far.

May you have warmth in your igloo,
Oil in your lamp, and peace in your heart.

• INUIT •

May your dreams ride on the wings of angels,
Who know their way home to the skies.

Never above, never below,
But always beside you.

Sclei g'ovar!
(May the King return!)

• SCOTTISH •

Sthastea!
(Happiness!)

• RUSSIAN •

Tante belle cose.
(So many beautiful things.)

• ROMA FANTON, ITALIAN •

To everybody in the whole wide, wide world,
Lest some damn fool thinks he has been overlooked.

The right time and place are coming for you,
Just don't let them pass!

Toast to the sunrise because you only have today,
And make the most of what you have,
For you don't know what tomorrow will bring.

We've holidays and holy days, and memory
days galore;
And when we've toasted every one, I offer just
one more.
So let us lift our glasses high, and drink a silent
toast—
The day, deep buried in each heart, that each one
loves the most.

Yarhamk Allah!
(May Allah bless you.)

• KUWAIT •

Generosity

Lift 'em high and drain 'em dry,
To the guy who says, "My turn to buy!"

May the winds of fortune go with you,
May you sail a gentle sea.
May it always be the other guy
Who says, "this drink's on me."

You cannot hold a torch to light another's path,
Without brightening your own.

Golf

Here's to the golfer who just missed a hole-in-one,
By six strokes!

To our golfer,
May he always be able to find his balls,
And may his putter never fail him.

To our golfer, may his investments always be
above par,
And his game always be below.

Good Fortune

May leprechauns dance over your bed,
And bring you sweet dreams.

• IRISH •

May the most you wish for,
Be the least that you get.

May the Lord keep you in the palm of His hand,
And never close His fist too tight upon you.

• IRISH •

May the rocks in your field all turn to gold.

• IRISH •

May you always have money in your pocket,
A woman to love,
And a smile on your face!

May your luck be like the capital of Ireland,
Always "Dublin."

• IRISH •

May your well never run dry.

Graduate

A toast to the graduate,
Who's in a class by himself!

Here's to the graduate,
Although your life in school is now complete,
The school of life is just beginning!

• JENNIFER RAHEL CONOVER •

Gratitude

Always try to do the right thing,
This will gratify some and astonish the rest!

To all of you who applauded,
For as the cow said to the farmer,
"Thanks for a warm hand on a cold morning!"

Greatness

Greatness is not in where we stand,
But in what direction we are moving.
We must sail sometimes with the wind and
sometimes against it,
But sail we must and not drift, nor lie at anchor.

• OLIVER WENDELL HOLMES •

Grocers

May we spring up like vegetables, have turnip noses,
Reddish cheeks and carroty hair,
And may our hearts never be hard like cabbages,
Nor may we be rotten to the core.

Guests

All our guests make us happy,
Some by coming and others by going.

Be not forgetful to entertain strangers,
For thereby some have entertained angels unawares.

Fill up, boys, to our royal guest,
The Prince of Good Fellows!

Happy to share with you such as we got,
The leaks in the roof, the soup's in the pot.
You don't have to thank us or laugh at our jokes,
Sit deep and come often, you're one of the folks!

Here's a toast to all who are here,
No matter where you're from,
May the best day you have seen,
Be the worst of those to come!

• CELTIC •

Here's to our guest,
Don't let him rest,
But keep his elbow bending,
'Tis time to drink,
Full time to think,
Tomorrow when you're mending.

The ornaments of your house,
Will be the guests who frequent it.

To our guest,
A friend of our friend's is doubly our friend.
Here's to him!

You are welcome here, be at your ease,
Get up when you're ready, go to bed when you
please!

Hangovers

Here's to the good time I can't remember!

• IRISH •

Happiness

Happy are we met,
Happy have we been,
Happy may we part,
And happy we meet again.

Happiness is good health and a bad memory.

• INGRID BERGMAN •

Happiness is like a kiss,
It feels best when you give it to someone else.

Here's a toast to happiness,
It sneaks in through a door you didn't know you
left open.

• JOHN BARRYMORE •

Here's to happy times,
May they come often and stay long!

Here's to long life and happiness,
For your long life will be my happiness.

May all your joys be pure joys,
And all your pain champagne.

May brooks and trees and singing hills
Join in the chorus, too,
And every gentle wind that blows
Send happiness to you.

May the joys of today,
Be those of tomorrow,
The goblets of life,
Hold no dregs of sorrow.

May your heart be warm and happy
With the lilt of sunny laughter,
Every day in every way
And forever and ever after.

May your thoughts be as glad as the shamrocks,
May your heart be as light as a song,
May each day bring you happy hours,
That stay with you all year long!

• IRISH •

May we be happy,
And our enemies know it!

• CELTIC •

Never forget that those who bring
Happiness to the lives of others
Cannot keep it from themselves.

• MAURICE MAETERLINCK •

The greatest happiness of life is the conviction that
we are loved,
Loved for ourselves, or rather in spite of ourselves.

• VICTOR HUGO •

The time to be happy is now,
And the place to be happy is here.

• ROBERT G. INGERSOLL •

To get the full value of joy, you must have someone
to divide it with.

• MARK TWAIN •

Hard Times

Clink, clink your glasses and drink,
Why should we trouble borrow?
Care not for sorrow,
A fig for the morrow,
Tonight let's be merry and drink.

Everybody in life gets the same amount of ice,
But the rich get it in summer and the poor in winter!

• BAT MASTERSON •

For the test of the heart is trouble,
And it always comes with years.
And the smile that is worth the praises of earth
Is the smile that shines through the tears.

Here's to a fellow who smiles
When life runs along like a song.
And here's to the lad who can smile
When everything goes dead wrong.

Here's to our friends in adversity,
And may we never be in the same fix.

Here's to you, my friend,
Wishing these hard times to mend.

If this is a blessing,
It certainly is well disguised.

• WINSTON CHURCHILL, ON HIS DEFEAT IN THE
1945 ELECTION •

It's easy to be pleasant when life flows by like a song.
But the man worthwhile is the one who can smile
When everything goes all wrong.

It's not as bad a world,
As some would make it,
But whether it's good or bad,
Depends on how you take it.

May the sunshine of comfort,
Shine through the gloom of despair!

May the thorns of life only serve
To give zest to its flowers.

May the winds of adversity
Ne'er blow open our door!

• SCOTTISH •

May you see each other through many dark days,
And make all the rest a little brighter.

May your troubles be less,
And your blessings be more,
And nothing but happiness,
Come through your door.

May we never do worse!

May we never feel want,
Nor ever want feeling.

The gem cannot be polished without friction,
Nor man perfected without trials.

The one who complains about how the ball bounces,
Is usually the one who dropped it!

There comes a time when you must take the bull by
the horns,
And face the situation squarely!

Troubles are like babies,
They grow larger by nursing them.

• HENRY WARD BEECHER •

We have been through the better and worse
(not always the better prevailed),
We've seen the richer and poorer
(the latter is most often sailed),
The sickness has outrun the health
(which often has caused much ado),
So now I pledge to you my heart,
'til death do us part,
And pray all our dreams will come true.

When my ship comes in,
I'll probably be waiting at the airport!

Within this goblet, rich and deep,
I cradle all my woes to sleep.

• TOM MOORE •

Health

Eat well, drink in moderation, and sleep sound,
In these three good health abounds.

Health and life to you,
Land without rent to you,
A woman of your choice to you,
A child every year to you,
A wet beak and may you die in Ireland!

• IRISH •

Health to my body, wealth to my purse,
Heaven to my soul and I wish you no worse.

• IRISH •

Here's a health to all those that we love,
Here's a health to all those that love us,
Here's a health to all those that love them that love
those,
That love them that love those that love us.

Here's health and prosperity,
To you and all your posterity,
And them that doesn't drink with sincerity,
May they be dammed for all eternity!

• IRISH •

Here's health to those I love,
And wealth to those who love me!

Here's to your good health,
And your family's good health,
And may you all live long and prosper.

• FROM "RIP VAN WINKLE," WASHINGTON IRVING •

Here's to your health,
You make age curious, time furious,
And all of us envious.

Here's wishing good health and long life to you,
And the choice of the girls for a wife to you,
And your land without penny of rent to you;
If these three blessing are sent to you,
Then there's peace and content to you.

• IRISH •

I wish you health,
I wish you wealth,
I wish you happiness galore,
I wish you heaven when you die,
What could I wish you more?

• CELTIC •

Joy, comfort and repose,
Slam the door in the doctor's nose.

• *POOR RICHARD'S ALMANACK* •

Salud, pesetas, y amor,
Y tiempo para gozarlos.
(Health, wealth, and love,
And time to enjoy them.)

• SPANISH •

Slaynt as shee as eash dy vea as maynrys son dy
bragh!
(Health and peace and age [length of life] and
happiness forever!)

• MANX •

Some friends wish you happiness,
And others wish you wealth,
But I wish you best of all,
Contentment blest with health!

The health of a salmon to you,
A long life, a full heart and a wet mouth!

• IRISH •

To your very good health,
May you live to be as old as your jokes.

While there's life on the lip,
While there's warmth in the wine,
One deep health I'll pledge,
And that health shall be thine.

Hell

Here's to Hell, may the stay there,
Be as much fun as the way there!

Here's to Mephisto! Goodness knows
What we would do without him.
And, good Mephisto, do not spurn
Our toast with mocking laughter,
Nor yet the compliment return
But toasting us hereafter.

• OLIVER HERFORD •

Here's to you and here's to me,
But should we ever disagree,
To hell with you and here's to me!

Here's to you two from we two,
For we two hope that you two,
Like we two as much as we two like you two,
But if you don't like we two,
Then to hell with you two and here's to we two!

May the grass grow long
On the road to hell
For want of use.

• IRISH •

Home

Home, the place where you're treated the best,
And grumble the most!

May (y)our house always be too small
To hold all (y)our friends.

• MYRTLE REED •

Mi casa es su casa!
(My house is your house!)

• SPANISH •

To home, where you can always find warm words on
a cold day!

To (y)our house and home,
Where there's a world of strife shut out,
And a world of love and peace shut in.

Hope

Dum spiro spero!
(While I breathe, I hope!)

• LATIN •

Never deprive someone of hope,
It may be all they have.

Nil desperandum!
(Never say die!)

• HORACE, LATIN •

Yesterday is but a dream, tomorrow is but a vision,
But today well lived makes every yesterday a dream
of happiness,
And every tomorrow a vision of hope. Look well,
therefore, to this day.

Hosts

A toast to our hosts
From all of us,
May they soon be the guests
Of each and every one of us!

Here's to the host and hostess,
We're honored to be here tonight,
May they both live long and prosper,
May their star of hope be ever bright.

Here's to our hostess, considerate and sweet,
Her wit is endless, but when do we eat?

Here's to the hostess and here's to the host,
As we raise up our glasses and offer this toast,
Thank you for this lovely meal,
Thank you for these friends so real,
Thank you for the way we feel,
We think you're just the most.

Nothing but the best for our hostess,
That's why she has us as friends.

One drink I can handle,
Two drinks at the most,
Three I'm under the table,
And four I'm under the host.

To our host, a most excellent man,
For is a man not fairly judged by the company
he keeps!

To our host, who makes us feel right at home,
Even though that's where he wishes we were!

To our hostess, who like a duck,
Is calm and unruffled on the surface,
And pedaling like hell underneath!

To the sun that warmed the vineyard,
To the juice that turned to wine,
To the host that cracked the bottle,
And made it yours and mine.

What is a table richly spread,
Without this woman at its head?
To our hostess.

Humor

A bumper of good liquor,
Will end a contest quicker
Than justice, judge or vicar,
So fill a cheerful glass,
And let good humor pass.

• RICHARD BRINSLEY SHERIDAN •

After a good dinner one can forgive anybody,
Even one's own relatives!

• OSCAR WILDE •

Always remember that hindsight is the best insight
to foresight.

An Irishman is never drunk as long as
He can hold onto one blade of grass,
And not fall off the face of the earth.

• IRISH •

A toast to the cocktail party where olives are speared,
And friends are stabbed!

As you ramble through life, whatever be your goal,
Keep your eye upon the doughnut, and not upon
the hole.

As you slide down the banister of life,
May the splinters never face the wrong way!

• CELTIC •

Bigamy means having one wife (husband) too many;
Some say monogamy means the same.
Good luck!

• CONFUCIUS •

Do you love me,
Or do you not?
You told me once,
But I forgot.

Frivolity is the species' refusal to suffer!

• JOHN LAHR •

Gentlemen, start your livers!

God grant me the senility
To forget the people I never liked anyway,
The good fortune to run into the ones I do,
And the eyesight to tell the difference!

God invented whiskey so the Irish wouldn't rule the
world!

• IRISH •

Grant me a sense of humor, Lord,
The saving grace to see a joke,
To win some happiness from life,
And pass it on to other folk.

Here's to a clear conscience,
   Or a poor memory!

Here's to a man after my own heart,
And after my house, and my wife. . . .

Here's to (bride) and (groom) who are like epoxy,
Separately they are perpetually sticky,
But together they form a permanent bond.

Here's to Eve, the mother of our race,
Who wore fig leaves in just the proper place.
And here's to Adam, the daddy of us all,
Who was Johnny-on-the-spot when the leaves began
   to fall.

Here's to you, you may not be as wise as an owl,
   But you're still a hoot!

Here's to the bride,
And here's to the groom,
And to the bride's father,
Who'll pay for this room.

Here's to the brilliant, warm, handsome (beautiful)
(pause)
Company that you keep!

I drink on occasion,
And sometimes when I have no occasion.

• MIGUEL DE CERVANTES •

I envy people who drink,
At least they know what to blame everything on.

• OSCAR LEVANT •

I feel just like a loaf of bread,
Wherever I go they toast me!

I know the things I know,
And do the things I do,
And if you do not like me so, to hell, my love, with
you!

• DOROTHY PARKER •

I used to know a clever toast,
But pshaw, I cannot think it,
So fill your glass to anything,
And bless your souls I'll drink it.

• WALLACE IRWIN •

I was always religiously inclined,
Said the oyster as he slid down the minister's throat,
But never did I dream I'd be entering the clergy.

I'd rather be with all of you,
Than with the finest people in the world.

I'd rather have a bottle in front of me
Than a frontal lobotomy.

If the soup had been as warm as the claret,
And if the claret had been as old as the bird,
And if the bird had had the breast of the parlor
maid who served it,
It would have been a hell of a fine dinner.

• STEVE COLHOUN •

In this world there are only two tragedies,
One is not getting what one wants,
And the other is getting it.

• OSCAR WILDE •

It doesn't matter where you get your appetite,
So long as you eat at home!

It is better to spend money like there's no tomorrow,
Than to spend tonight like there's no money.

• P. J. O'ROURKE •

Lord, fill my mouth with worthwhile stuff,
And nudge me when I've said enough!

May the bloom of the face never extend to the nose.

May you get it all together,
Before you come apart!

May you live until a dead horse kicks you!

• GYPSY •

Never eat more than you can lift!

• MISS PIGGY •

Oh, life is a glorious cycle of song,
A medley of extemporanea,
And love is a thing that can never go wrong,
And I am Marie of Romania.

• DOROTHY PARKER •

Over the teeth and past the gums,
Look out, stomach, here it comes!

Please, my dear, don't criticize,
I know my faults are many,
And although you're very wise,
Are you sure you haven't any?
For a better mate you often sigh,
You tear me all asunder,
But were I perfect,
Would I have chosen you, I wonder?

Remember that no matter how thin you slice it,
There are always two sides.

Surely, a fine husband is he that flinches
At the mere raisin' of his wife's fair hand.

• CELTIC •

The reason the Welsh (Scottish, Irish) are always
fighting each other
Is because they have no other worthy opponents!

• CELTIC •

There is only one thing in this world
Worse than being talked about,
And that is not being talked about.

• OSCAR WILDE •

To hay fever, here's looking at-chooo!

To you, the second most supportive element in my life,
I wish I could say you were the first,
But at my age I'm not about to go braless.

To nouveau riche,
It's better than no riche at all.

You can always tell an Irishman
But you can't tell him much!

• IRISH •

Husbands

Here's to that most provoking man,
The man of wisdom deep,
Who never talks when he takes his rest,
But only smiles in his sleep.

Here's to the man who loves his wife,
And loves his wife alone,
For many a man loves another man's wife,
When he ought to be loving his own!

Here's to the man who won not just my heart,
But also my mother's approval.

To husbands, American women expect to find in
them a perfection
That English women only hope to find in their
butlers.

To the model husband,
Any other woman's!

Ideas

It takes only a singe idea
And a single action to change the world.

To genius, which is merely the ability
To reduce the complex to the simple.

Imagination

A mind once stretched by an original idea
Never returns to its original size.

Only those who can see the invisible
Can do the impossible.

Immediacy

Carpe diem!
(Seize the day!)
• LATIN •

Nunc aut nunquam!
(Now or never!)

• LATIN •

Toast to the sunrise because you only have today,
And make the most of what you have,
For you don't know what tomorrow will bring.

Ireland

Ireland, it's the one place on earth,
That heaven has kissed
With melody, mirth,
And meadow and mist.

Ireland, sir, for good or evil,
No other place under Heaven,
And no man can touch its sod,
Or breathe its air without becoming
Better or worse.

Now sweetly lies old Ireland,
Emerald green beyond the foam,
Awakening sweet memories,
Calling the heart back home.

Kindness

Have you had a kindness shown?
Pass it on,
'Twas not given for you alone,
Pass it on.
Let it travel down the years,
Let it wipe another's tears,
'Til in heaven the deed appears,
Pass it on.

No act of kindness, no matter how small, is ever
wasted.

• AESOP •

Kiss

Drink to me only with thine eyes,
And I will pledge with mine;
Or leave a kiss within the cup,
And I'll not look for wine.

• BEN JONSON •

Here's headfirst, in a foaming glass!
Here's headfirst, to a lovely lass!
Here's headfirst, for a bit of kissing,
For the good don't know the fun that they're
missing!

Here's some food for thought,
I heard it at a recent ball,
'Tis better to be kissed and caught,
Than never to be kissed at all.

Here's to a kiss:
Give me a kiss, and to that kiss add a score,
Then to that add a hundred more;
A thousand to that hundred, and so kiss on,
To make that thousand quite a million.
Treble that million, and when that is done,
Let's kiss afresh as though we'd just begun.

Here's to the lasses we've loved, my lad,
Here's to the lips we've pressed,
For kisses and lasses, like liquor in glasses,
The last is always the best.

May we kiss those we please,
And please those we kiss!

They say there're microbes in a kiss,
This rumor is most rife.
Come, dear lady, and make me an invalid for life!

Lawyers

Do as adversaries in law,
Strive mightily, but eat and drink as friends.

• WILLIAM SHAKESPEARE •

Here's to my lawyer, a man of great trials
And many convictions.

Here's to the law,
A bad compromise beats a good lawsuit.

Here's to the lawyer, a bright gentleman,
Who rescues your estate from your enemies,
And keeps it for himself.

Here's what my lawyer taught me—
Say it with flowers,
Say it with eats,
Say it with kisses,
Say it with sweets,
Say it with jewelry,
Say it with drink,
But be careful, never, never say it with ink!

To lawyers, you cannot live without the lawyers,
And certainly you cannot die without them.

• JOSEPH H. CHOATE •

Leadership

Leaders are like eagles, they don't flock,
You find them one at a time.

To our leaders,
There are millions of birds in the sky,
But very few are eagles!

Life

Bis vivit qui bene vivit!
(He lives twice who lives well!)

• LATIN •

Dance as if no one were watching,
Sing as if no one were listening,
And live every day as if it were your last.

Dum vivimus vivamus.
(While we live let us live.)

• TOAST OF THE EPICUREANS, FOLLOWERS OF EPICURUS,
LATIN •

Here's to life,
A long headache in a noisy street!

Here's to a long life and a merry one,
A quick death and an easy one,
A pretty girl and a true one,
A cold bottle and another one.

If you love life, do not squander time,
For that is the stuff life is made of.

• BENJAMIN FRANKLIN •

Life, alas, is very drear.
Up with the glass and down with the beer!

Life consists not in holding good cards,
But in playing those you hold well.

Life is like a cup of tea,
It's all in how you make it!

Make life last
As long as it's worth living.

Make the most of life while you may,
For life is short and wears away!

May the joys of today be those of tomorrow,
And the goblets of life hold no dregs of sorrow.

• ESTELLE FOREMAN •

May thy life be long and happy,
Thy cares and sorrows few,
And the many friends around thee,
Prove faithful, fond and true.

May we live respected and die regretted.

May you always be tender with the young,
Compassionate for the old,
And tolerant of the weak,
Because at one time or another in life,
You will have been all of these.

To life! The first half is ruined by our parents,
The second half by our children!

To life, where each moment is a turning point,
And opportunities swarm thicker than gnats at
sundown.

• HENRY VAN DYKE •

To life, where sometimes what appears to be the end
Is really a new beginning!

To the tides of life,
Which are sometimes very rough,
But each storm makes us,
A better Captain of our soul!

Vita brevis, ars longa.
(Life is short, art is long.)

• LATIN •

We don't remember the days of our life,
We remember the moments.

We make a living by what we earn,
And we make a life by what we give.

Yesterday is just a dream, tomorrow but a hope,
Look to today, for it is life!

Literary

Let's hear it for our propagandists,
The people who bring us the news,
Unburdened by troublesome scruples,
They're proud of their compromised views,
There once was a time we admired them,
We thought they were principled fighters,
But what we see now is more worthy,
Of the Union of Soviet Writers.
That they should be liberty's guardians,
Is truly a shame and a pity,
These shills and these flacks,
These stooges and hacks,
These sold-out scribes,
Who report on the tribes,
Who rule from our capital city.
Let's hear it for commentators,
Those masters of punditry,
Who share with us all their opinions,
Which range from A to B,
Standing right there in the spotlight,
They could do some significant things,
But we'd sooner expect a puppet,
To dance without sticks or strings;
Impressing no one but their colleagues,

They're not even clever or witty,
These shills and these flacks,
These stooges and hacks,
These sold-out scribes,
Who report on the tribes,
Who rule from our capital city.
Let's hear it for all those reporters,
Who learn how the game is played;
If they will just write what's expected,
They can be handsomely paid,
But most garner practically nothing,
And eventually fall off the ladder;
The losers depart mostly wiser while the winners
grow gradually sadder;
Let's hear it for all these survivors,
Whose road to the top is not pretty,
These shills and these flacks,
These stooges and hacks,
These sold-out scribes,
Who report on the tribes,
Who rule from our capital city.

• DAVID MARTIN •

A book is like a garden carried in the pocket.

There is no frigate like a book
To take us lands away.

• EMILY DICKINSON •

Love

Amantium irae amoris integratio est.
(Lovers' quarrels are the renewal of love.)

• TERENCE, LATIN •

Amor vincit omnia.
(Love conquers all.)

• LATIN •

Because I love you truly,
Because you love me, too,
My very greatest happiness
Is sharing life with you.

Brew me a cup for a winter's night,
For the wind howls loud and the furies fight,
Spice it with love and stir it with care,
And I'll toast your bright eyes, my sweetheart fair.

• MINNA THOMAS ANTRIM •

Come in the evening, or come in the morning,
Come when you are looked for, or come without
warning,
A thousand welcomes you will find here before you,
And the oftener you come here, the more I'll adore
you.

Cras amet qui nunquam amavit,
Quique amavit, cras amet.
(May he love tomorrow who has never loved before,
And may he who has loved, love tomorrow as well.)

• LATIN •

Drink for faith and hope is high,
None so true as you and I,
Drink the lover's litany,
Love like ours can never die!

Here's to Dan Cupid, the little squirt,
He's lost his pants, he's lost his shirt,
He's lost most everything but his aim,
Which shows that love is a losing game!

Here's to love and unity,
Dark corners and opportunity!

Here's to love,
To those who seek it,
May they find it.
To those who've found it,
May it be everlasting.

• NICK ADDAMS •

Here's to love, the only fire for which there is no
insurance!

Here's to love, which is nothing
Unless it's divided by two!

Here's to one and only one,
And may that one be,
One who loves but one and only one,
And may that one be me!

Here's to the girl I love,
And here's to the girl who loves me,
And here's to all those who love her whom I love,
And all those who love her who love me.

Here's to the girl I love the best,
It ought not to be hard to guess it,
For I raise my glass and gaze at one,
Who loves me but won't confess it.

Here's to the girl that's good and sweet,
Here's to the girl that's true,
Here's to the girl that rules my heart,
In other words, here's to you.

Here's to the love that I hold for thee,
May it day by day grow stronger,
May it last as long as your love for me,
And not one second longer!

Here's to the water,
Wishing it were wine,
Here's to you, my darling,
Wishing you were mine.

Here's to the wings of love,
May they never molt a feather,
Till my big boots and your small shoes,
Are under the bed together!

Here's to thee and thy folks from me and my folks,
And if thee and thy folks love me and my folks,
As much as me and my folks love thee and thy folks,
Then there never was folks since folks was folks,
That love me and my folks as much as thee and
thy folks.

Here's to those that I love best,
Here's to those that love me,
Here's to those that love those that I love,
And to those that love those that I love.

Here's to those who love us,
And here's to those who don't,
A smile for those who are willing to,
And a tear for those who won't.

Here's to those who'd love us,
If we only cared,
Here's to those we'd love,
If we only dared!

I have known many,
Liked a few,
Loved only one,
So here's to you.

If the ocean were a goblet,
And all its salt seas wine,
I would drink it to you, darlin',
Ere you cross the foamy brine;
For then you couldn't cross it,
But would have to stay on land,
Till the walkin' should get better,
And we'd cross it hand in hand!

Love cometh like sunshine after the rain.

• WILLIAM SHAKESPEARE •

Love does not consist in gazing at each other,
But in looking outward in the same direction.

• ANTOINE DE SAINT-EXUPERY •

Love doesn't make the world go round,
But it sure makes the ride worthwhile!

• MAE WEST •

Love is the greatest refreshment in life.

• PABLO PICASSO •

Love is the only game not called
On account of darkness.

May love draw the curtain,
And friendship the cork.

May the feelings of love never fade,
Once felt they are forever made,
Expressions may differ with the years,
But true love endures the final years.

May those now love,
Who never loved before,
May those who have loved,
Now love even more

May you always share your love and laughter.

May you live in love forever,
And may love live forever in you.

May you never ever have lived,
May you never ever have loved,
So that good drink
Will ever make you think,
You might have done better.

May your life bring love,
May your love bring life!

May your love be like the wind,
Strong enough to move the clouds,
Soft enough to never hurt,
But always never-ending.

May we have the unspeakable good fortune
To win a true heart, and the merit to keep it.

May we have those in our arms
Whom we love in our hearts.

Men want to be a woman's first love,
Women have a more subtle instinct,
What they want is to be a man's last romance.

The love you give away is the only love you keep!

• ELBERT HUBBARD •

There is no surprise more magical than
The surprise of being loved,
It's God's finger on man's shoulder.

• CHARLES MORGAN •

To every lovely lady bright,
I wish a gallant faithful knight;
To every faithful lover, too,
I wish a trusting lady true.

• SIR WALTER SCOTT •

To love, which is like quicksilver in the hand.
Leave the fingers open and it stays in the palm,
Clutch it and it darts away.

• DOROTHY PARKER •

To us, we may not have it all together,
But together we have it all!

When you love someone set him (her) free,
If he (she) runs away,
Hunt him (her) down and kill him (her).

When the roaring flames of your love
Have burned down to embers,
May you find that you've married your best friend.

Where love is concerned
Too much is never enough.

Women love with all their heart,
And men love with all their strength.

Luck

A jolly good smoke, a nicely turned joke,
A handful of trumps when at play,
A drop of old wine, champagne that's fine,
And a run of good luck from today!

For each petal on the shamrock,
This brings a wish your way,
Good health, good luck, and happiness,
For today and every day.

• IRISH •

Here's luck, and a drop to wet your whistle.

• RICHARD HOVEY •

Here's luck, great luck,
Such luck as ne'er was known,
May the winner's pockets bulge with coin,
And these pockets be . . . my own!

I would tell you good luck,
But I never wish luck on a sure thing.

May Dame Fortune ever smile on you,
But never her daughter, Miss Fortune.

May he (she) get all he (she) wishes but one,
So he (she) will always have something to strive for!

May the luck of the Irish
Lead to happiest heights,
And the highway you travel
Be lined with green lights.

• IRISH •

May the luck of the Irish possess you,
May the devil fly off with your worries,
And may God bless you forever and ever!

• IRISH •

May your blessings outnumber
The shamrocks that grow,
And may trouble avoid you
Wherever you go.

• IRISH •

No amount of planning can ever replace dumb luck!

Wherever you go and whatever you do,
May the luck of the Irish be there with you.

• IRISH •

Luxury

Give me the luxuries of life,
And I can dispense with the necessities.

Let us drink to the luxuries of life,
If we have those, we can disperse
With the necessities!

Marriage

A happy marriage is still the greatest treasure within
the gift of fortune.

Don't forget that marriage is like maintaining your
motor home,
Change the oil, tune it up, and don't forget to polish
it once in a while.

Down the hatch to a striking match!

Happy marriages begin when we marry the one we
love,
And they blossom when we love the one we
married!

• SAM LEVENSON •

Here's to a second marriage, the triumph of hope
over experience!

• SAMUEL JOHNSON •

Here's to marriage, one soul in two bodies.

Here's to marriage, the high sea for which no
compass has yet been invented!

• HEINRICH HEINE •

Here's to marriage, which is a lot like the army,
Everyone complains but you'd be surprised
By the large number that reenlist!

• JAMES GARNER •

Here's to marriage, which they say is give and take,
These days if a man doesn't give his wife enough she
takes it!

Keep your marriage brimming,
With love from the loving cup,
Whenever you're wrong, admit it,
Whenever you're right, shut up!

• OGDEN NASH •

Marriage is a wonderful institution,
But who wants to live in an institution!

• GROUCHO MARX •

Marriage is the alliance of two people,
One of whom never remembers birthdays,
And the other who never forgets.

• OGDEN NASH •

Marriages are all happy,
It's having breakfast together that causes all the trouble!

May your home be filled with laughter,
And all your dreams come true,
May marriage always hold
The best of everything for you.

May your marriage be like a mighty ship,
Always holding a true and steady course,
Weathering rough seas with strength and courage,
And sailing calm waters with style and grace.

May your marriage be modern enough to survive
the times,
And old-fashioned enough to last forever!

Remember that if you ever put your marital
problems on the back burner,
They're sure to boil over.

Seek a happy marriage with wholeness of heart,
But do not expect to reach the Promised Land
Without going through some wilderness together!

The honeymoon is the vacation a man takes
Before starting work under a new boss!

To Marriage: A community consisting of a master,
a mistress,
And two slaves—making in all, two.

• AMBROSE BIERCE •

To marriage, an institution very like a tourniquet,
Because it stops your circulation.

To marriage, which resembles a pair of scissors,
So joined they cannot be separated,
Often moving in opposite directions,
Yet punishing anyone who comes between them.

• SYDNEY SMITH •

To marriage, which is made in heaven,
But don't forget, so are thunder and lightning!

To the two secrets to a long-lasting happy marriage,
Here's to a good sense of humor and a short memory!

Men

Before marriage, a man will lie awake all night
Thinking about something you said,
After marriage, he'll fall asleep
Before you finish saying it.

• HELEN ROWLAND •

Here's to men,
If they had hot flashes,
You can bet there'd be estrogen in the water supply!

Here's to the man who takes a wife,
May he make no mistake,
For it makes a lot of difference,
Whose wife it is you take.

Here's to the man who is wisest and best,
Here's to the man who with judgment is blest,
Here's to the man who's as smart as can be,
I mean the man who agrees with me.

Here's to the married man,
He could have made many women happy by
remaining a bachelor,
And he also could have made one woman happy by
remaining a bachelor!

Here's to the men of all classes,
Who through lasses and glasses,
Will make themselves asses.

Here's to the men, God bless them!
Worst of my sins I confess them,
Is loving them all, be they great or small,
So here's to the boys, God bless them!

Here's to the men that we love,
Here's to the men that love us,
The men that we love aren't the men who love us,
So the hell with the men and here's to us!

Here's to the working man,
Hunger may look in his door,
But it dares not enter.

To man, give him an inch
And he thinks he's a ruler!

To men, who divide our time,
Double our cares, and triple our troubles.

To the men I've loved,
And the men I've kissed,
My heartfelt apologies to the men I've missed!

Women's faults are many, men have only two,
Everything they say and everything they do!

Military

God grant me the eyes of an eagle, the radar of a bat,
And the balls of an Army helicopter pilot!

Here's to a bloody war and a quick promotion.

Here's to a young lady named Banker,
Who slept while the ship lay at anchor,
She awoke in dismay,
When she heard the mate say,
Now hoist up the topsheet and spanker!

Here's to fighting, feasting and fornicating!

• MARINES •

Here's to our sailors, long may they ride the waves!

• NAVY •

Here's to sea room
And a willing foe!

• BRITISH NAVY •

Here's to the army and the navy,
And the battle they have won,
Here's to America's colors,
The colors that never run.

Here's to the girl that lives on the hill,
She won't but her sister will!

Here's to the girls from Norfolk,
They neither drink nor smoke Nor . . . folk!

• NAVY •

Here's to the Navy, true hearts and sound bottoms!

Here's to the ships of our Navy,
And the ladies of our land,
May the first be well rigged,
And the latter well manned!

• NAVY •

Here's to the soldier and his arms,
Fall in, men, fall in,
Here's to woman and her arms,
Fall in, men, fall in.

• ARMY •

Here's to us,
And men like us,
Too damn few of us left!

• ARMY •

I give you muscles of steel, nerves of iron, tongues
of silver,
Hearts of gold, necks of leather, the Marines.

Success to our army, success to our fleet,
May our foes be compelled to bow down at our feet.

To long lives and a short war!

• COLONEL POTTER ON *M*A*S*H* •

To our wives and sweethearts,
May they never meet!

• NAVY •

To our women, our horses, and the men who ride
them.

• A U.S. CAVALRY TOAST FROM WWI •

To the ships of our oceans and the women of our
land,
May the former be well captained and the latter be
well manned!

• BRITISH NAVY •

Millennium

Raise your glass high!
2000 bubbles, one for each year.
Round like the world, promising good cheer.
A tribute to mankind for all we've achieved.
To the courage and sacrifice of those who believed.
Good-bye to a millennium, hello to a new.
Here's to the pleasure of beginning with you!

• DAVID AKERS •

For this worldwide celebration,
Let us offer up a small libation,
With this golden nectar let us toast,
Those we care about the most!

• JENNIFER RAHEL CONOVER •

May the best of this year,
Be the worst of the next.

• IRISH •

Now that the witching hour is nigh,
Let us raise our glasses high,
We offer up the gods a toast,
For those we care about the most,
Here's peace, health, love, and cheers,
And miracles to follow in the coming years!

• JENNIFER RAHEL CONOVER •

Since it's almost the millennium,
Toasts will flow ad "infinit-i-um,"
Let's hope we all remember,
From now until at least December,
To make the world a better place,
For the entire human race!

• JENNIFER RAHEL CONOVER •

Miners

May all your labors be in vein!

Ministers

To the ministers who don't preach,
And the preachers who minister.

Miracles

Never give up on anyone or anything,
Miracles happen every day.

Mistakes

Here's to mistakes,
Learn from those of others,
You may not live long enough,
To make them all yourself!

May our faults be written on the seashore,
And every good deed be a wave to wash them out!

Moderation

Here's to temperance—in moderation!

Here's to the temperance supper,
With water in glasses tall,
And coffee and tea to end with,
And me there not at all.

Let us acknowledge the evils of alcohol,
And strive to eliminate the wine cellar,
One glass at a time.

"Lips that touch liquor shall never touch mine,"
Thus cried the maiden with fervor divine,
But from her statement what must we infer—
They shan't touch her liquor, or shan't touch her?

• WILLIAM SHAKESPEARE •

Take the glass away,
I know I hadn't oughter,
I'll take a pledge, I will,
I never will drink water!

• W. E. P. FRENCH •

Mothers

Congratulations, we all knew you had it in you!

• DOROTHY PARKER (TO A NEW MOTHER) •

Here's to the best years of my life,
Spent in the arms of another man's wife . . . my
mother!

I drink to one
Whose image never may depart,
Deep graven on this grateful heart,
My mother!

It's not the woman with ebon locks,
Nor the one with head of brown,
Nor the lady fair with the golden hair,
Nor the one with the copper crown,
But the woman I love best of all,
And the one I toast tonight,
With her smiling face and easy grace,
Wears a mane of shimmering white, my mother.

To our fathers' sweethearts,
Our mothers!

To our mothers, God bless them every one,
May the eyes of the fathers and the love of the sons,
Watch over and protect them, keep them holy and
pure,
With life to sustain and health to endure.

To the mother who bore me,
There's no one more bold,
She's dearer by far
Than all the earth's gold.

Mountain Man

Here's to the childs (children) what's come afore,
Here's to the pilgrims what's come arter (after),
May your trails be free of griz (grizzly bear),
And your packs filled with plews (beaver pelts),
And fat buffler (buffalo) in your pot!

• Sam Arnold •

Nature

To nature, which is the art of God.

See Nature, and through her, God.

Nautical

Bottoms Up!

• A classic toast, but not one to ever give a
sailor! •

Dear Lord above,
Send down a dove,
With wings as sharp as razors,
To cut the throats of them thar' blokes
Whot sell bad beer to sailors!

Embrace poverty with dignity,
Go sailing!

Fair winds, smooth seas and a safe voyage home!

Here's to having a drink on the rocks in a boat,
Rather than having a boat on the rocks in the drink!

Here's to learning the ropes
Without coming unraveled!

Here's to yachting,
It's not just a matter of life and death,
It's a lot more important than that!

May your happiness be as deep as the ocean,
And your sorrows as light as the foam!

May all your landfalls be expected!

• JOHN KETTLEWELL •

May your voyage through life be happy and free,
As the dancing waves on the deep blue sea.

The standing toast that pleased me the most was,
The wind that blows, the ship that goes,
And the lass that loved a sailor!

• BRITISH NAVY •

There are good ships, and there are wood ships,
The ships that sail the sea,
But the best ships, are the friendships,
And may they always be!

New Year's

A song for the old, while its knell is tolled,
And its parting moments fly!
But a song and a cheer for the glad New Year,
While we watch the old year die!

• GEORGE COOPER •

Another year is dawning, let it be true,
For better or for worse, another year with you.

As we start the New Year,
Let's get down on our knees
To thank God we're still on our feet!

• IRISH •

Be at war with your vices,
At peace with your neighbors,
And let every New Year find you a better man.

• BENJAMIN FRANKLIN •

Here's a toast to the future,
A toast to the past,
And a toast to our friends, far and near,
May the future be pleasant,
The past a bright dream,
May our friends remain faithful and dear.

Here's to the bright New Year,
And a fond farewell to the old,
And here's to the things that are yet to come,
And to memories that we hold!

May all your troubles in the coming year
Be as short-lived as your New Year's resolutions!

May this year be the best you've ever had,
And the worst of those to come!

• IRISH •

May your nets be always full,
Your pockets never empty.
May your horse not cast a shoe,
Nor the devil look at you in the coming year.

• IRISH •

Ring out, wild bells, to the wild, wild sky,
The year is dying in the night,
Ring out wild bells, and let him die.
Ring out the old, ring in the new,
Ring out the false, ring in the true.

• ALFRED, LORD TENNYSON •

Welcome be ye that are here,
Welcome all, and make good cheer,
Welcome all, another year!

Opportunity

May you learn to listen well,
Opportunity sometimes knocks very softly.

Small opportunities are often the beginning of great
achievements.

The bump in the road is either an obstacle to be
overcome,
Or an opportunity to be enjoyed,
It is entirely up to you.

When one door closes, another opens,
Seize the opportunity while the pathway is lit!

Optimism

Here's to optimism, where every obstacle
Is but a stepping-stone to your success.

Patience

Patience is a virtue, believe it if you can,
It's seldom found in woman and never in a man.

Peace

Here's to health, peace, and prosperity,
May the flower of love never be nipped by the frost
of disappointment,
Nor the shadow of grief fall among a member of this
circle.

May our leaders be wise, and our commerce increase,
And may we experience the blessings of peace.

Mir i druzhba.
(Peace and friendship.)

• RUSSIAN •

Pax vobiscum.
(Peace be with you.)

• LATIN •

Perseverance

In the battle between the stream and the rock,
The stream always wins,
Not through strength, but through perseverance.

To perseverance, the ability to move mountains,
One grain of sand at a time.

Philosophy

Here's to philosophy,
A route of many roads leading
From nowhere to nothing!

Pilots

May all your takeoffs equal your landings.

Politicians

Here's to our politicians who, like the streets of
Washington,
Just keep going round in circles!

Here's to the honest politician who,
Once he's bought, stays bought.

Here's to the politician, a person who divides his time
Between running for office and running for cover.

Here's to the politician, a person who straddles the issue
When he isn't dodging one.

Postal Workers

To postal workers,
They deliver letters everywhere,
Even the cemetery, Dead Letters!

Poverty

Here's to poverty,
It sticks to a man when all his friends forsake him!

May poverty always be a day's march behind us.

• IRISH •

Remember the poor, it costs nothing.

• JOSH BILLINGS •

Praise

If all your marvels one by one,
I'd toast without much thinking,
Before the tale was well begun,
I'd be dead from drinking!

Press

A health to the slaves of the ink-pot,
Who, careless of fortune or fame,
Will give their best years,
Missing brilliant careers,
And all for the love of the game!

• JAMES P. HAVERSON •

To the journalist who tries to get into places
Other people are trying to get out of.

Procrastination

To procrastination, which has saved me from
innumerable mistakes.

Professors and Education

Let schoolmasters puzzle their brain,
With grammar and nonsense and learning,
Good liquor, I stoutly maintain,
Gives genius a better discerning.

• OLIVER GOLDSMITH •

Now here's to Addition,
Another pint, pray!
Then here's to Subtraction,
Take the old one away!
Here's Multiplication,
So double the wine!
And here's to Division,
That's yours, and this mine!

• WALLACE RICE •

To our professor,
A woman who talks in her students' sleep.

To our professor,
Addition to your friends,
Subtraction from need,
Multiplication of your blessings,
Division among your foes.

Prohibition

Four and twenty Yankees,
Feeling very dry,
Went across the border
To get a drink of rye,
When the rye was opened,
The Yanks began to sing,
Not *God bless America*,
But *God Save the King*!

• CANADIAN TOAST DURING PROHIBITION •

Here's to Carry Nation,
Of antidrink renown,
Who, though against libation,
Hit ev'ry bar in town!

Here's to Prohibition,
The devil take it!
They've stolen our wine,
So now we make it!

Prosperity

May the morning of prosperity shine on the evening
of adversity.

• IRISH •

May your feast days be many,
And your fast days be few.

• IRISH •

To a prosperous individual,
From what I understand,
He doesn't count his money, he measures it.

When climbing the hill of prosperity,
May we never meet a friend coming down!

Psychiatrists

To my psychiatrist,
He finds you cracked,
And leaves you broke.

To the psychiatrist,
A person who doesn't have to worry
As long as other people do.

Retirees and Retirement

Here's to the Retiree, who knows everything
And has plenty of time to tell you all about it!

To retirement, which is a mixed blessing,
You get twice as much husband
And half the money!

Risk

A ship in the harbor is safe,
But that's not what ships were made for!

Risqué

A friendly glass and a friendly lass always go well
together,
But a friendly lass with a friendly ass always go
even better,
So, here's to the glass and the lass with the ass,
May all three be found together!
We'll drink the glass and feel the ass
And make all three feel much better!

Be careful, the toes you step on today
Could be connected to the ass
You kiss tomorrow.

Friends may come,
Friends may go,
Friends may peter out, you know,
But we'll be friends through thick or thin,
Peter out or peter in.

God made you a lady,
God made you beautiful,
God made you charming,
God made you lovely,
And oh, God, I wish I could!

God made woman and made her out of lace,
He didn't have enough so he left a little space,
God made man and made him out of string,
He had a little left so he left a little thing.

Here's a toast for the game of twenty toes,
It's played all over town,
The women play with toes turned up,
And the men with toes turned down!

Here's hoping you always cheat, steal and lie,
Cheat the devil, steal away from bad company and
lie next to the one you love!

Here's to a girl, she is so sweet,
Makes things stand that have no feet!

Here's to a man named Skinner,
Who took his wife out to dinner,
By 9:00 P.M. it was in her.
Not Skinner, the dinner.
Skinner was in her before dinner!

Here's to a young lady of Kent,
Who said that she knew what it meant
When men asked her to dine,
Gave her cocktails and wine.
She knew what it meant, but she went!

Here's to all of the women who have used me and
abused me . . .
And may they continue to do so!

Here's to heat,
Not the kind that ignites and burns down shanties,
But the kind that excites and brings down panties!

Here's to honor,
Once you're honor, stay on her!

Here's to it, and to it again,
If you don't do it when you get to it,
You may never get to it to do it again!

Here's to my girlfriend, who answers the door in
her nighty,
When she stands between the window and me,
Great Lord a-mighty!

Here's to nipples,
Because breasts would be so pointless without them!

Here's to rape, riot, and revolution,
May sex prosper, prostitution flourish,
and sunnavabitch become a household word!

Here's to the breezes that blow through the treeses,
That blow the skirts off of young girls' kneeses,
Which lead to the sights that sometimes pleases,
But more often leads to social diseases.

Here's to the bull that roams the wood,
He does the heifers lots of good,
If it wasn't for the road he trod,
What would we do for beef, by God?

• REDD FOXX •

Here's to the girl in the high button shoes,
She spends my money and drinks my booze,
I've given her bracelets and a big diamond ring,
She sleeps with her mother, the stingy old thing!

Here's to the girl in the little green shoes,
She takes your money and she drinks your booze,
She has no cherry but that's no sin,
She's still got the box the cherry came in.

Here's to the girl that I love best,
I've seen her naked and I've seen her dressed,
I've done it standing and I've done it lying,
If I had wings I'd do it flying.

Here's to the girl who's inclined to be wild,
Three things prevent her from becoming beguiled,
The love of dear Jesus,
The dread of diseases,
And the fear of becoming with child.

Here's to the girl who's made of wood,
I would have made her if I could,
Because I liked her and she liked me,
But only God can make a tree!

Here's to the girl with the high silk hat,
Open-weave stockings and French cravat,
Black lace gloves and a pink parasol,
Poor little pussy paid for it all!

Here's to the lady all dressed in black,
She always looks forward and never looks back,
And when she kisses she kisses so sweet,
She makes things stand that haven't got feet!

Here's to the love of my life,
And here's also to his wife!

Here's to the mouse on the mantelpiece,
That stuck his tail in the candle grease,
You must admit he didn't have much class,
But he was the only mouse with a French-fried ass!

Here's to the Virgin Mary, who conceived without
sinning,
So that we may sin without conceiving!

Here's to the woman that clings like a vine,
Blooms every month and bears every nine,
The only creature between heaven and hell,
Who can extract juice from a nut,
Without cracking its shell!

Here's to you and for you and to you again,
If I hadn't met you it wouldn't have been,
But since I met you and I let you,
I bet you if I meet you, I'll let you do it again!

Here's to you and here's to me,
And here's to love and laughter,
I'll be true as long as you, but not a minute after!

Here's to you and me,
Two pairs of shoes upon a chair,
Two pairs of pants are also there,
A hug, a kiss, a sigh,
Hush, hush, someone's coming — is it you or I?

Here's to you because I love you,
I love you because you're good,
You're good because God made you,
God, how I wish I could!

Here's your top to my top (touch glass tops),
Your bottom and my bottom (touch bases),
Your middle and my middle (touch middles),
I like you so much I'm going to give you a little!
(pour a bit into the other glass)

Here's to your eyes, Here's to my eyes.
Here's to your thighs, Here's to my thighs.
Our eyes have met, our thighs not yet.
But here's hoping!

Here's to your wife and your horse,
May you mount them often and forever.

Here's to teeny, teeny boys
With great big expensive toys.

• KIM NAIMOLI •

I love them, all the ladies,
With their frilly little things.
I love them with their diamonds,
Their perfumes and their rings.
I love them, all the ladies,
I love them big and small,
But when a lady isn't quite a lady,
That's when I love them most of all.

I'll toast the girls who do,
I'll toast the girls who don't,
But not the girls who say they do and later say
they won't,
But the girl I'll toast from the break of dawn to the
wee hours of the night,
Is the girl who says I never have, but for you I might.

I'll toast to the ones that will,
I'll toast to the ones that won't,
but I won't toast to the ones who say they will,
And later say they won't!

May I never be above you,
May I never be below you,
But always in you!
(At this point the person reciting the toast pours a
bit of his drink into the other person's glass)

May the itching piles caress you,
And corns grow on your feet,
And crabs as big as lobsters crawl up your balls
and eat,
And when the day of Judgment comes,
And you're a sympathetic wreck,
May you fall through your own arsehole,
And break your Goddamn neck.

• CLAYTON B. BUTLER •

May your wedding night be like a kitchen table,
Four legs and no drawers!

• IRISH •

Non corber indum illegitimie.
(Don't let the bastards get you down.)

• LATIN •

On the chest of a barmaid in Sale,
Were tattooed the prices of ale,
And on her behind,
For the sake of the blind,
Was the same information in Braille!

Saludos, pesetas,
Y mujeres con grande te-yetas!
(Health, money, and women with large mammaries!)

• TEX-MEX •

She offered a toast,
He offered his honor,
And all night long,
He was on-er and off-er.

Si jeunesse savait, si vieillesse pouvait!
(If the young only knew, if the old only could!)

• FRENCH •

There once was a prince from Ioda,
Who wouldn't pay a whore what he owed her,
So with much savoir faire she stood on a chair,
And peed in his whiskey and soda!

To the perfect girl I found at last,
I could not ask for more,
She's deaf, dumb, oversexed,
And owns a liquor store!

Today's the day, tonight's the night,
We've shot the stork, so you're all right!

We drink to the men who are big,
We drink to the men who are small,
We drink to the men who say they are big,
But really aren't at all.
But the men we raise our glasses to,
In the middle of the night,
Are the men who go from small to big,
And slide in just right!

When we're toes to toes my nose is in it,
When we're nose to nose my toes are in it,
And when I'm in I've got no one to talk to!

• (WEDDING TOAST WITH A VERY SHORT GROOM
AND A VERY TALL BRIDE) •

St. David's Day

St. David's Day is an enchanted time,
A day to begin transforming winter's dreams
Into summer magic!

• WELSH •

St. Patrick's Day

May the Leprechauns be near you to spread good
luck along your way,
And may all the Irish angels smile upon you St.
Patrick's Day!

• IRISH •

St. Patrick was a gentleman,
Who through strategy and stealth,
Drove all the snakes from Ireland,
Here's toasting to his health,
But not too many toastings,
Lest you lose yourself and then,
Forget the good St. Patrick,
And see all those snakes again!

• IRISH •

Salesmen

Here's to opening accounts and closing deals!

Here's to us,
Never sell a salesperson short.

Song

Here's a health to the King and a lasting peace,
To factions' end and wealth increase.
Come let us sing it while we have breath,
For there's no singing after death.

• EIGHTEENTH-CENTURY TOASTING SONG •

Let us sing our own treasures, Old England's
good cheer,
To the profits and pleasures of stout British beer;
Your wine tippling, dram-sipping fellows retreat,
But your beer-drinking Britons can never be beat.
The French with their vineyards and meager pale ale,
They drink from the squeezing of half-ripe fruit;
But we, who have hop-yards to mellow our ale,
Are rosy and plump and have freedom to boot.

• ENGLISH DRINKING SONG, CIRCA 1757 •

Why, we'll smoke and drink our beer,
For I like a drop of good beer, I does,
I'ze fond of good beer, I is,
Let gentlemen fine sit down to their wine,
But we'll all of us here stick to our beer.

• OLD SOMERSETSHIRE ENGLISH SONG •

Sorrow

We cannot share this sorrow,
If we haven't grieved a while,
Nor can we feel another's joy,
Until we've learned to smile.

Speakers

Here's to our speaker,
May his speech be like a pencil and have a point.

To our speaker,
May he rise to the occasion and sit down soon
thereafter!

We'll bless our toastmaster,
Wherever he may roam,
If he'll only cut the speeches short,
And let us all go home.

Spoonerism

Raise your arses to the queer old dean!
(Should be "Raise your glasses to the dear old
Queen!")

• REVEREND WILLIAM SPOONER •

Stockbrokers

Here's to the stockbroker,
He can tell you what's going to happen next month
to your money,
And later explain why it didn't.

Here's to the stockbroker,
May your life be full of bulls!

To the stockbroker, a capitalist,
Who invests himself with other people's money.

Success

Dreams give one wings,
Dare to soar and succeed.

Here's success and wealth,
May it be exceeded only by love and good health!

• JENNIFER RAHEL CONOVER •

Here's to success,
It's vastly easier to go down the hill than up,
But the view is so much better from the top!

Here's to success, some only dream of it,
While others get up and work hard at it.

Here's to success, which is only a journey,
Not a destination.

Here's to your success,
Success is like a very heady wine,
But you handle yours just fine!

No one can predict to what heights you will soar,
Not even you will know until you spread your wings.

Some measure success by their wealth,
But real success you cannot spend,
It's the way your child speaks of you
When talking to a friend.

Some people only dream of accomplishing great
things,
Others get up and do them!

The difference between successful individuals and
others
Is not a lack of knowledge but a lack of will.

The key to happiness is having dreams,
And the key to success is making your dreams come
true.

To success, and the road to it,
Which is always under construction.

To success, do not follow where the path may lead,
But go ahead where there is no path and leave a
trail.

To success,
Never let defeat have the last word.

To success,
Unless you try something beyond what you already
know,
You will never grow.

Teamwork

Here's to teamwork, the thing that allows
Common people to achieve miraculous results!

It is a fact that in the right formation,
The lifting power of many wings
Can achieve twice the distance of
One bird flying alone.

Never doubt that a small group of committed people
Can change the world,
Indeed it's the only thing that ever has.

None of us are as strong as all of us!

To teamwork: snowflakes are one of nature's most
fragile creations,
But look what they can do when they stick together.

Tennis

Here's to tennis,
The sport where love means nothing.

Here's to those who have the guts to be in the tennis
racket.

To tennis, may we all have net gains.

Thanksgiving

Here's to the turkey I'm about to eat,
And the turkeys I'll eat it with.

The American eagle and the Thanksgiving turkey,
May one give us peace,
And the other a piece for all our plates.

Thrift

Beware of little expenses,
A small leak can sink a large ship!

• BENJAMIN FRANKLIN •

Sumptus censum ne superet.
(Live within your means.)

• LATIN •

To thrift and our ancestors who practiced it,
So that we don't have to!

Travel

A vacation is what you take
When you can no longer take what you've been
taking.

• EARL WILSON •

Before taking steps the wise man knows
The object and end of his journey.

• W. E. B. DU BOIS •

Not traveling is like living in the Library of
Congress,
But never taking out more than one or two books.

• MARILYN VOS SAVANT •

One of the great joys of life
Is being up at first light
And setting out on empty roads to go somewhere
difficult and significant!

The next best thing to being rich is traveling
As though you were.

• STEPHEN BIRNBAUM •

The vagabond, when rich,
Is called a tourist.

• PAUL RICHARD •

To travel, for traveling, especially traveling light,
Teaches you the difference between what is
necessary in life
And what may be an onerous burden.

• RICK BERG •

To traveling, what matters is the trip,
And the sights along the way.

• ELIZABETH FORSYTHE HAILEY •

The further you go, the more you shall see and know.

Valentine's Day

To my Valentine,
I love you not only for what you are,
But what I am when I am with you.

Victory

Here's to victory, which only happens
When ten thousand hours of training
Meet one moment of opportunity.

Let's have a drink,
Let's have some fun,
Because at last,
The job is done.

Turn failure into victory,
Don't let your courage fade,
And if you get a lemon,
Just make lemonade.

Vincam aut moriar!
(I will conquer or die!)

• LATIN •

Vincit qui se vincit.
(We must first learn to conquer ourselves.)

• LATIN •

Virtue

Be to your virtues a little kind,
Be to your faults a little blind!

Wales

The problem with Wales (Scotland, Ireland) as I see it
Is that it's a country full of genius
But with absolutely no talent!

• CELTIC •

There are two kinds of people on this earth,
The Welsh (Irish, Scottish) and those who wish they
were.

• CELTIC •

To Wales, the only country in which the expected
never happens,
And magic and enchantment are commonplace.

• JENNIFER RAHEL CONOVER •

Wales is rich in literature that understands a soul's
yearning,
And dancing that understands a happy heart!

War

Aut vincere aut mori!
(Victory or death!)

• (ROMAN TOAST BEFORE GOING OFF TO BATTLE, LATIN) •

Qui desiderat pacem praeparet bellum.
(Let him who desires peace prepare for war.)

• LATIN •

Wealth

Here's to the almighty dollar,
Without which we would have no cents.

Weddings

A song is not a song until it's sung,
A bell is not a bell until it's rung,
Love is not love until it's given away,
And today (bride's name) and (groom's name) have
given their love to each other,
While sharing it with all of us, let us drink to their
happiness.

A toast to love and laughter,
And happiness ever after!

As you write a new chapter in your life as husband
and wife,
May your union be like a game of poker,
Start as a pair and end up with a full house!

(Bride's name) and (groom's name);
A case of love pure and simple,
(Bride's name) is pure and (groom's name) is simple.

(Bride's name), please place your hand on the table,
(Groom's name), please place your hand on your
bride's,
Now I want everyone to see the last time that
(Groom's name) has the upper hand.

By all means marry; if you get a good wife,
You'll become happy; if you get a bad one,
You'll become a philosopher.

• SOCRATES •

Coming together is a beginning,
Keeping together is progress,
Working together is success.

• HENRY FORD •

Gorko, gorko.
(Bitter, bitter.)

• TRADITIONAL RUSSIAN BOYAR WEDDING TOAST—THE
GUESTS ALL CHANT IT SO THE BRIDE AND GROOM WILL KISS
AND MAKE THE WINE "SWEET." •

Here's a toast to the lovely bride,
And to the husband by her side,
Here's a toast to the home they're going to share,
May love and trust dwell with them there.

Here's hoping this wedding ring will serve as a
tourniquet to stop your circulation.

Here's to a night of sweet repose,
Tummy to tummy and toes to toes,
One brief moment of sheer delight,
Then it's fanny to fanny the rest of the night!

Here's to my mother-in-law's daughter,
Here's to her father-in-law's son;
Here's to the vows we've just taken,
And the life we've just begun.

Here's to the bride and the bridegroom,
We'll ask their success in our prayers,
And through life's dark shadows and sunshine,
That good luck may always be theirs.

Here's to the groom, a man who's kept his head
Even though he lost his heart.

Here's to the groom with bride so fair,
And here's to the bride with groom so rare!

Here's to the health of the happy pair,
May good luck meet them everywhere,
And may each day of wedded bliss,
Be always just as sweet as this.

Here's to the husband and here's to the wife,
May they remain lovers for the rest of their life.

Here's to you who halves my sorrows
And doubles my joys.

Here's to your happy launching of the Court Ship
On the sea of Matrimony.
May the rocks be confined to the cradle!

Here's to the bride that is to be,
Here's to the groom she'll wed,
May all their troubles be light as bubbles
Or the feathers that make up their bed!

Here's to this fine couple,
May their joys be as bright as the morning,
And their sorrows but shadows that fade in the
sunlight of love.

Here's to the newlyweds,
May your being together,
Be a joy forever and ever.

It is written that when children find true love,
Parents find true joy,
Here's to your joy and ours,
From this day forward!

Let us raise our glasses,
And then imbibe,
To the splendid couple,
Who founded this tribe.

Let us toast to the health of the bride,
Let us toast to the health of the groom,
Let us toast to the person that tied,
Let us toast every guest in the room!

• WILLIAM SHAKESPEARE •

Live long; fight fair!

Look down, you gods,
And on this couple drop a blessed crown.

• WILLIAM SHAKESPEARE •

Love, be true to her, Life, be dear to her,
Health, stay close to her, Joy, draw near to her,
Fortune, find what you can do for her,
Search your treasure house through and through
for her,
Follow her footsteps the wide world over,
And keep her husband always her lover.

• ANNA LEWIS •

May all your t̶
And may you both live
For all the days of y̶

               • IRISH •

May all your ups and downs be only in bed!

May God be with you and bless you,
May you see your children's children,
May you be poor in misfortune, rich in blessings,
May you know nothing but happiness from this day
forward.

               • IRISH •

May God bless you both
And keep your hearts as one.

May the special moments of today,
Be the most remembered memories of tomorrow.

May you always love each other more than yesterday,
But less than tomorrow.

...y you both grow old upon one pillow.

May you live long lives,
Doing what you love, together,
And when the time comes for you to pass away,
May you die as you lived,
Doing what you love, together.

May your hands be forever clasped in friendship,
And your hearts forever joined in love.

• CELTIC •

May your hearts be open with patience and love,
May your lives be filled with blessings from above,
May you always share the best that life can provide,
As you spend your life together side by side.

May your life together generate sufficient clouds,
Only to make a glorious sunset!

May your love be as endless as your wedding rings.

May your marriage be like a fine wine,
Getting better and better with age.

May your wedding days be few,
And your anniversaries be many!

• CELTIC •

May the roof over us never fall in,
And may we friends gathered below never fall out.

• IRISH •

May the sparkle in your eyes
Light your path for the years to come.

May the two of you breakfast with Health,
Dine with Friendship, crack a bottle with Mirth,
And sup with the goddess of Contentment.

May the sun shine upon you, lighting your way,
So that darkness may leave and perish today.

May you be poor in misfortune and rich in blessings,
May you be slow to make enemies and quick to
make friends,
But, rich or poor, quick or slow,
May you know nothing but happiness from this day
forward.

• IRISH •

May your eyes stay filled with stars,
And your heart with visions of dreams yet to come.

Nothing is nobler, nor more admirable,
Than when two people who see eye to eye,
Live together as husband and wife,
Thereby confounding the enemy and delighting their
friends!

• HOMER •

Now you will feel no rain, for each of you will be
shelter to the other,
Now you will feel no cold, for each of you will be
warmth to the other,
Now there is no loneliness for you, for each of you
will be companion to the other,

Now you are two persons with one life before you,
Go now to your dwelling to enter into the days of
your life together,
And may your days be good and long upon the
earth.

• APACHE WEDDING BLESSING •

The knot was tied, the couple wed,
And then the smiling bridegroom said unto the
preacher,
Shall I pay the usual fee today or would you have me
wait a year,
And then give you 100 clear,
If I should find the wedding state,
As happy as I estimate.
The preacher lost no time in thought,
To his reply no study brought,
There were no wrinkles on his brow,
He said, "I'LL TAKE THREE DOLLARS NOW!"

There are three rings in the circle of life,
The engagement ring, the wedding ring and the
suffer-ring!

To the happy couple on this (month, e.g., June) night,
May you never go to bed angry, after a fight!

To my wife,
My bride and joy!

To the bride and groom,
May they have a lifetime of love,
And an eternity of happiness.

To the newlyweds,
May "for better or worse" be far better than worse.

Two such as you with such a master speed,
Cannot be parted nor be swept away,
From one another once you are agreed,
That life is only life forevermore,
Together wing to wing and oar to oar.

• ROBERT FROST •

Wedlock's like wine,
Not properly judged until the second glass.

• ERNEST JARROLD •

With trumpets and fanfare,
I wish you the happiest of all days.

Wine and Spirits

After the third cup,
Wine drinks the man!

• BUDDHIST SANSKRIT TEXT •

A book of verse beneath the bough,
A jug of wine, a loaf of bread, and thou.

• RUBAIYAT OF OMAR KHAYYAM •

A warm toast,
Good company and a fine wine,
May you enjoy all three.

• IRISH •

Any port in a storm, or any other wine for that
matter!

Before our fading years decline,
Let us quaff the brimming wine.

• SIGN IN A LONDON PUB •

Drink! for you know not whence you came, nor why,
Drink! for you know not why you go, nor where.

• RUBAIYAT OF OMAR KHAYYAM •

Fill his glass to the brim!
Round the table let it roll.
The divine says that wine,
Cheers the body and the soul.

Fill up, boys, and drink a bout,
Wine will banish sorrow,
Come drain the goblet out,
For we'll have more tomorrow.

Give me wine to wash me clean
From the weather-stains of care.

• RALPH WALDO EMERSON •

God, in his goodness, sent the grapes,
To cheer both great and small,
Little fools will drink too much,
And great fools none at all.

Good company, good wine,
Good welcome make good people.

• WILLIAM SHAKESPEARE •

He who clinks his cup with mine,
Adds a glory to the wine.

• GEORGE STERLING •

Here's to mine and here's to think!
Now's the time to clink it!
Here's a flagon of old wine,
And here we are to drink it.

Here's to the thirst that is yet to come.

• CELTIC •

Here's to whiskey oh so clear,
Just like a woman's lips, but more sincere.

In water one sees one's own face;
But in wine one beholds the heart of another.

• FRENCH •

It is best to rise from life as from the banquet,
Neither thirsty nor drunken.

• ARISTOTLE •

Let us have wine and women, mirth and laughter,
Sermons and soda water the day after.

• LORD BYRON •

Old wood to burn,
Old wine to drink,
Old friends to trust,
And old authors to read.

• FRANCIS BACON •

Pour deep the rosy wine,
And drink a toast with me,
Here's to the three,
Thee, wine, and camaraderie!

• TOM MOORE •

The Frenchman loves his native wine,
The German loves his beer,
The Englishman loves his 'alf and 'alf,
Because it brings good cheer;
The Irishman loves his "whiskey straight,"
Because it gives him dizziness;
The American has no choice at all,
So he drinks the whole damn business.

To you and yours, and theirs and mine,
I pledge with you their health in wine.

• IRISH •

To wine, which is nothing less than bottled poetry!

• SIGN IN A LONDON PUB •

When wine enlivens the heart,
May friendship surround the table.

Wine comes in at the mouth,
And love comes in at the eye,
That's all we shall know for truth,
Before we grow old and die,
I lift the glass to my mouth,
I look at you, and I sigh.

• WILLIAM BUTLER YEATS •

Wine improves with age,
I like it more the older I get!

Wisdom

The wise adapt themselves to circumstances,
As water moulds itself to the pitcher.

Wasser macht weise
Froelich der Wein
Darum trinke beides
Um beides zu sein!
(Water makes you wise
Wine makes you glad
So drink them both
In order both to be!)

• GERMAN •

Wine, wit, and wisdom,
Wine enough to sharpen the wit,
Wit enough to give zest to the wine,
And wisdom enough to quit at the right time!

Wisdom is knowing what road to follow,
And integrity is having the strength to take it!

Wonder is the beginning of wisdom.

Wives

A health to our widows,
If they ever marry again may they do as well!

• IRISH •

A good wife and health
Are certainly a man's best wealth!

Here's to the lovely woman I fought to marry at
any cost,
The struggle was worth it, without her I'd be lost.

To my wife and our anniversary,
Which I forgot once but never will again!

To my wife,
Here's to the prettiest, here's to the wittiest,
Here's to the truest of all who are true,
Here's to the nearest one, here's to the sweetest one,
Here's to them, all in one, here's to you!

Women

A liberated woman is one who has sex before
marriage
And a job after.

• GLORIA STEINEM •

A wise woman puts a grain of sugar into
Everything she says to a man,
And she takes a grain of salt
With everything he says to her.

Be bold in what you stand for,
And careful what you fall for.

Drink to fair woman, who, I think,
Is most entitled to it,
For if anything can drive me to drink,
She certainly could do it.

Here's to God's first thought, Man!
Here's to God's second thought, Woman!
Second thoughts are always best,
So here's to women!

Here's to our sweethearts and our wives,
May our sweethearts soon become our wives,
And our wives ever remain our sweethearts.

Here's to the maiden of bashful fifteen,
Here's to the widow of fifty,
Here's to the flaunting, extravagant queen,
And here's to the housewife who's thrifty.

Here's to the woman, my sweetheart and wife,
She's never done anything wrong in her life.
It took me some time, for my soul I did fear,
But finally I learned this lesson most dear.

Here's to the woman that's good and sweet,
Here's to the woman that's true,
Here's to the woman that rules my heart,
In other words, here's to you.

Here's to woman, the fair magician,
Who can turn man into a donkey and make him feel
like a lion.

Here's to woman, who only needs four animals to
make her happy,
A jaguar in her garage,
A mink on her back,
A tiger in her bed,
And a jackass to pay for it all!

Here's to women, the ultimate aristocrats,
They elect without voting, govern without law,
And decide without appeal.

Let her be clumsy, or let her be slim,
Young or ancient, I care not a feather,
So fill up a goblet, fill it to the brim,
Let us toast all the ladies together.

Let the toast pass, drink to the lass,
I'll warrant she'll prove an excuse for the glass.

• RICHARD BRINSLEY SHERIDAN •

May our wine brighten the mind,
And strengthen our resolution.

May your liquor be cold,
May your women be hot,
And may your troubles slide off of you
Like it or not!

There's two theories to arguing with a woman.
Neither one works!

To the first woman, who if the legend be true,
Was only a side issue.

To woman, she needs no eulogy,
She speaks for herself!

To woman,
A paradox who puzzles when she pleases,
And pleases when she puzzles.

What, sir, would the people of the earth be without
women,
They would be scarce, sir, almighty scarce.

• MARK TWAIN •

Who loves not women, wine and song,
Remains a fool his whole life long.

• JOHN HENRY VOSS •

Work

Do what you love,
And may we always love what we do.

• HENRY DAVID THOREAU •

May the work that you have
Be the play that you love.

• E. GEBERDING •

Writers and Writing

Here's to the writer,
For although truly democratic,
He still keeps in touch with "royalty"!

Nunc scripsi totum pro Christo da mihi potum!
(Now, I have written so much for Christ, give me a
drink!)
Monk-copyists marked the end of a manuscript with
this inscription

• LATIN •

Orator fit, poeta nascitur!
(Orators are made, poets are born!)

• LATIN •

Acknowledgments

Thanks to all the many contributors to this book; it wouldn't have been possible without you. My heartfelt apologies if I've forgotten anyone!

Nick Addams
Sam Arnold, Owner, Fort
    Restaurant, Denver, CO
Barbara Ashley
David Athey
Ralph Baker
Peg and Harry Bancroft
Don Barnes
Bill Barr
Charlie Bascombe
Kathleen and Bernard Beck
Alan Bell
Betty Van Berckelaer
Dan Berger
Pongsuwan Bilmes
Fred Black
Nina Black

Jean Charles Bloch
James Bluck
Barbara and Dave Bluto
Cy Bluto
Carole and David Boyd
Nancy and Hank Brefka
B. J. Buntrock
Jeanette and Bob Burke
Jo Ann Bussa
James R. Campey
John Caproni
Bob Carey
Nancy Carmichael
Janet Casias
Fritz Caughron
Richard Choinski, Captain
    of *Sea Cloud*

Pearce Coady
Chris and Martin Conn
Ted Conover
Richard Cook
William Crow
Patricia Cunnington
Sandi Davids
The Honorable Joseph E.
  Davies
Rahel Davies
Donald Dewey
Chris Deyong
Tom Diack
Sharon and Harry Dickson
Ernie and Maggie Doud Jr.
Lloyd Dryer
John Dulany
Sally Dumfries
Sheila Dunlop
Perry Duryea
Juanita Eastman
Sean Eckford
Joan and Jimmy Edwards
Paulina Gerchov and Aaron
  Einikhovich
Ann Ellison
Prescila Espiritu
Deborah Estévez
Jim and Linda Evans

Emlen Davies Evers
Rick Eyerdam
Roma Fanton
Kevin Farr
Sally Fisher
Burdette Mase Fitch
Joanne and Keith Fitch
Joyce and John Flaherty
Stephanie Fletcher
Maryan Floyd
Nancy and Allen Forbes
Steve Forrester
James Fournier
K. Franssen
Margie and Morgan French
George Gaganis
Gay Gahagan
Richard Gale
Loy Gernert
Paula Gibbs
Liz Gill
Larry Gilley
Ellen Glasser
Bob Gordon
Ginny Goshdigian
David and Louise Granger
Tom Graves
Lisa Greenberg
Barbara Greenspun

Emyr Griffith
Marilyn and Fred Guardabassi
Johanna Hall
Colette and Dan Hanley
Sam Harrison
Neesa Hart
Kedric and Suzie Hasha
Richard Heard
Roland Heiler
Kathy and Ray Heimbecker
Jerry Herriman
Topsy High
Dusty Hilliard
Meakin Hoffer
Ken Hogg
Shirley and Jerry Huber
Florence and Jack Hutton
Bobbie and Bill Jacobson
Mike Jarrett
Jack Jennings
Curt Jensen
Agnes and Tom Johnson
Arthur Johnson
Sarah and Tony Jones-Lloyd
Gerri, Angelo, and Marla
    Karaliolios
Jack Kelly
Tom Kenney
Sean Kirwin

Katherine Kozul
Madeleine and George
    Lambert
Tove U. Lange
Marion Langston
Father Harry Lawson
Jonathan Leifer
Tochia and Stan Levine
Anna Lewis
Gerhard Lickfett, Captain of
    Star Flyer
Chuck Lininger
Sandra Lopez
Nell MacCracken
Thérèse and Ken Maggio
Thelma Maltz
Bob Marks
Clare Marlowe
David Martin
George Martin
John Mayer
Bernard McCormick
Joette and Dan McCully
Betty and Hamish
    McGregor
Sean McGregor
George McIver
Marie and Oliver McKeag
Shane McKeever

David McMahon
Scot McTigue
Nick Messinger
Bodil Millberg
Michael Miller
Lorenzo Monaco
Christer Mörn, President
    Sea Cloud Cruises
George Moxon
Jim and Joyce Munro
Nola and Brian Murphy
Dr. Leonard Muschaweck
Menahi Al Mutairi
Kim and Steve Naimoli
Art Nicely
Manny Nicholaides
Rosie and Walter Nielson
Bernice and Dave Nixon
Betty and Pres Northcutt
Anne Odom
Stephanie Olson
Dorsey Patrick
Gene Pecoraro
Maricela Pena
Louis Philippe
Preston Pitts, Jr.
Flip and Dieter Pohl
Vladislav V. Potapov
Alan and Marian Price

Ginny and Dan Probert
Doak Procter IV
Cathy Rae
Bob Rafner
Manuel Ramirez, Former
    Chief of Protocol to the
    OAS
Teresity Ramos
Martha Reed
Bernard Reilley
Sally Renberg
Marianne and Jorge
    Ricardez
Freda Richardson
Bernard Rielley
Marc Rikmenspoel
Austin Ross
Tim Ruth
Dominic Santarelli
Meryl Sawyer
Kevin Schmidt
Kendall Schrader
Tonya and Bill Schultz
Ted Shank
Holly Sherwood
Jodie Silverman
Chris Spohr
Hildegarde Sterling
Nancy and Chuck Stoll

Sara Stolzenberg
Connie and Mel Sylvan
Esther Sylvan
Lotta and Chris Sylvan
Ginger Tatoul
Helen Taylor
Pattie and Bob Toler
Maria Toriello
Bill Townsend
Lowell C. Trott
Melody A. Trott
John Tunney
Penny Turtle
Stanley Urban
Noel Vassallo
Annemarie and Michael
    Victory
Marietjie and Pieter van der
    Walt
Beth Wainwright
Mary Walker

Dean Andrew Waller
Bob Walton
Sam Warner
Julie Watson
Michael and Ellis Weatherly
Carolyn Weaver
Lynda and Alex Weiss
Bolte and Bill Wellington
Anne Wenner
Fee and Dennis Weston
Ed Wheelock
Stuart A. Whitlock
Patricia Wickman
Bogumila Wieclaw
Chuck Williams
Daniel E. Williams
Marianne Willman
Suzanne Walker Wright
Bill Wychulis
Vanda and Jim Yonge

Index

Absent Friends 15

Accountants 17

Acheson, Dean 59

Action 17

Actors 18

Adams, Franklin 64

Addams, Nick 175

Addison, Joseph 105

Adolescence 19

Adventure 19

Advertising 20

Advice 20

Aesop 162

Afrikaans 116

Age 20, 51,136

Agents 27

Akers, David 196

Aldrich, Henry 89

Alimony 27

Ambition 28

America 28, 102

Amphis 85

Anniversary 30, 253

Antiques 32

Antrim, Minna Thomas 173

Apache 255

April Fools' Day 32

Architects 33

Aristotle 260

Armenian 252

Army 194, 195

Arnold, Sam 202

Athletes 33

Attitude 33

Babies 34, 63

Bacall, Lauren 58

Bachelors and Bachelorettes 37, 82

Bacon, Francis 260

Bakers 38

Baldness 38

Bankers 39

Barrymore, John 133

Beaumont, Francis. 86

Beauty 39

Beecher, Henry Ward . . . 139

Beer and Ale. 39, 67, 69, 81, 168, 227, 232

Berg, Rick 240

Bergman, Ingrid 132

Best Wishes 44

Better Times 45, 80, 215

Biblical. 102, 105, 115

Bierce, Ambrose. 33, 82, 189

Billings, Josh 211

Birnbaum, Stephen. 240

Birthdays 47

Blacksmiths 49

Blessings 13, 50, 76, 108, 184, 252, 255

Bogart, Humphrey 56

Bosses 54

British Navy. 193, 204

Britt, Stuart Henderson 20

Browning, Robert 22

Buddhist 257

Builders 54

Burns, Robert 84

Butler, Clayton B. 227

Byron, Lord 35, 92, 260

Canadian 119, 214

Carter, Hodding 63

Cavalry 195

Celebration 55

Celebrities 16, 19, 22, 29, 32, 33, 50, 52, 55, 61, 62, 65, 76, 78, 85, 86, 87, 88, 89, 90, 91, 92, 99, 103, 104, 105, 108, 114, 115, 118, 130, 132, 133, 134, 135, 136, 137, 144, 145, 149, 151, 153, 154, 155, 156, 158, 163, 168, 169, 175, 179, 181, 182, 183, 186, 187, 189, 190, 196, 200, 202, 205, 213, 221, 227, 233, 239, 240, 246, 256, 258, 259, 261, 265, 269

Celtic 13, 14, 15, 26, 34, 35, 48, 62, 64, 67, 75, 94, 109, 110, 131, 134, 142, 150, 157, 243, 252, 253, 259

Cervantes, Miguel de 153

Challenges 60

Champagne 60, 133

Chaucer, Geoffrey 77

Children. 62, 251

Chimney Sweeps 63

Choate, Joseph H. 166

Christening 63

Christmas 64

Churchill, Winston 56, 137

Clans 69, 96

Coaches. 70

Colhoun, Steve 155

Colombian. 117

Confucius 150

Congratulations. 70

Conover, Jennifer Rahel 27, 94, 129, 196, 197, 234, 243

Coolidge, Calvin 82

Cooper, George. 205

Copeland, Bill 115

Cotton, Charles 87, 92

Courage. 71

Cousins 69

Creativity. 72

Creditors 72

Critics 72

Curses 73, 94, 227

Davis, Bette 58

Death and the Departed 75, 85, 86, 90, 91, 244

Decatur, Stephen. 16

Defeat 71, 79

Dentists 80

Designing Women 59

Dickens, Charles 28, 66

Dickinson, Emily. 172

Diller, Phyllis. 58

Diplomats 81

Discretion 82

Divorce 83

Doctors and Medicine 83

Dominican Republic 116, 122

Dowling, Bartholomew 76

Dreams. 84, 124, 254

Drink 39, 84, 105, 109, 148, 153, 154, 180, 212

Drunkenness 92

Du Bois, W. E. B. 239

Dyer, John 114

Ecclesiastes 102, 105

Editors. 94

Egerton, John 118

Emerson, Ralph Waldo 76, 258

Enemies 12, 56, 74, 94
Entrepreneurs 95
Epicurus 55, 167
Eternity 95
Excellence 95
Fairweather, J. H. 65
Family 69, 96, 149
Fanton, Roma 125
Farewells 96
Farmers 97, 115, 129
Fathers 98
Fields, W. C. 56
Firemen 98
Fishing 99, 108
Fletcher, John 85, 86
Focus 101
Food 101, 105, 154,
155
Ford, Henry 246
Foreman, Estelle 168
Fourth of July 102
Foxx, Redd 221
Franklin, Benjamin 168,
205, 238
Freedom 44, 103
French 90, 104, 228,
260
French, W. E. P. 200
Friendship 15, 21, 45,

47, 53, 62, 65, 89, 97,
103, 123, 136, 145, 165,
179, 182, 204, 209, 252,
262
Frost, Robert 59, 256
Future 114
Gambling 114
Gardening 115, 130
Garner, James 187
Geberding, E. 269
General 9, 115
Generosity 126
Genius 160
German 118, 263
Goldsmith, Oliver 60,
213
Golf 127
Good Fortune 127
Graduate 129
Gratitude 129
Greatness 130
Greek 55, 113
Grocers 130
Guests 130
Guiness, Sir Alec 57
Gypsy 156
Hailey, Elizabeth Forsythe
240
Hangovers 132

Happiness....... 102, 125, 132, 142, 235, 251

Hard Times 46, 135

Hassoldt, W. L. 41

Haverson, James P. 212

Health....... 83, 112, 140, 230, 231, 234, 248, 264

Heine, Heinrich....... 186

Hell 143

Herford, Oliver 61, 144

Holbrook, Hal........ 59

Holmes, Oliver Wendell 21, 29, 130

Home 145

Homer.............. 254

Honor 44

Hope............... 146

Horace.......... 89, 146

Hosts.............. 147

Hovey, Richard 183

Howe, Julia Ward 108

Hubbard, Elbert 181

Hugo, Victor 135

Humor 13, 16, 18, 20, 24, 25, 36, 39, 40, 42, 55, 56, 61, 64, 81, 87, 93, 112, 114, 118, 123, 129, 147, 148, 149, 165, 175, 179, 186, 187, 192, 193, 194, 195, 196, 200, 203, 204, 215, 216, 237, 243, 245, 255, 256, 257, 261, 263, 265, 267, 268

Hupfeld, Herman 57

Husbands 159, 245

Ideas 160

Imagination 160

Immediacy........... 160

Ingersoll, Robert G...... 135

International 9

Inuit................ 124

Ireland 94, 140, 161, 227

Irish 12, 14, 15, 21, 22, 23, 24, 43, 44, 46, 48, 52, 53, 67, 68, 69, 73, 74, 76, 77, 91, 93, 100, 104, 108, 110, 111, 116, 117, 120, 121, 127, 128, 132, 134, 140, 141, 143, 144, 150, 151, 158, 183, 184, 185, 197, 205, 206, 211, 215, 227, 230, 251, 253, 254, 257, 261, 264

Irving, Washington 141

Irwin, Wallace 154

Italian 125

Jarrold, Ernest........ 256

Jefferson, Thomas 57

Johnson, Ben 26, 163

Johnson, Samuel 186

Jung, Carl 59

Kennedy, John F. 56, 59

Kennedy, Rose 57

Kettlewell, John 204

Khayyam, Omar . . . 257, 258

Kilpatrick, James J. 78

Kindness 162

Kipling, Rudyard . . . 90, 108

Kiss 84, 163

Kuwait 126

Lahr, John 151

Latin 28, 40, 45, 75,
    77, 80, 89, 117, 119, 146,
    160, 161, 167, 170, 173,
    174, 209, 227, 238, 242,
    244, 270

Lawyers 149, 165

Leadership 166

Levant, Oscar 153

Levenson, Sam 186

Lewis, Anna 250

Life 167

Literary 171

London, Jack 19

Longfellow, Henry Wadsworth
    75

Love 107, 109, 173,
    241, 250, 262

Lowell, James Russell . . . . .
    90

Luck . . 48, 52, 116, 128, 183

Luxury 185

Mabie, Hamilton Wright . . . .
    65

Maeterlinck, Maurice . . . . . .
    134

Manx 142

Marines 193

Marquis, Don 25, 99

Marriage 108, 185

Martin, David 172

Marx, Groucho . . . 55, 88, 187

Masterson, Bat 136

Men 159, 190

Mexican 116, 117

Military 192

Millennium 196

Miners 197

Ministers 198

Miracles 198

Miss Piggy 156

Mistakes 198

Moderation 199

Moore, Tom 139, 261

Morgan, Charles 181

Mothers 200
Mountain Man 202
Naimoli, Kim 225
Nash, Ogden 91, 187
Nature 202
Nautica 51, 170, 186,
　　188, 202, 248
Navy 193, 194, 195,
　　196, 204
Neaves, Lord 42
New Year's 205
Nigeria 41
Opportunity 207
Optimism 208
O'Rourke, P. J. 155
Parker, Dorothy 62,
　　85, 154, 156, 182, 200
Patience 208
Peace 208
Perserverance 209
Picasso, Pablo 179
Philosophy 210
Pilots 210
Polish 24
Politicians 210
Poor Richard's Almanac 142
Pope, Alexander 55
Postal Workers 211
Potter, Colonel 195

Poverty 211
Praise 212
Press 212
Procrastination 213
Professors and Education
　　213
Prohibition 214
Prosperity 15, 215
Psychiatrists 216
Rabelais, Francois 56
Reed, Myrtle 145
Retirees and Retirement
　　216
Rice, Wallace 213
Richard, Paul 240
Risk 217
Risqué 18, 23, 29,
　　42, 97, 148, 152, 191, 192,
　　217
Robbins, John 52
Rochefoucauld, Duc de la
　　104
Rowland, Helen 190
Runaway Bride 58
Russian 121, 125,
　　209, 246
Saint-Exupery, Antoine de
　　179
Salesmen 230

Scott, Sir Walter 181
Scott, Willard 56
Scottish 13, 98, 122,
    125, 137, 157, 243
Shakespeare, William . . . . .
    165, 178, 199, 250, 259
Sheridan, Richard Brinsley
    149, 267
Smetana, Bedrich 43
Smith, C. O. Mrs. 88
Smith, Sydney 189
Socrates 113, 246
Song 231
Sorrow. 232
Spanish 115, 116,
    117, 122, 142, 145
Speakers 232
Spock, Mr. 57
Spooner, Reverend William
    A. 233
Spoonerism 233
St. David's Day 229
St. Patrick 52
St. Patrick's Day 230
Steinem, Gloria 265
Sterling, George 259
Stevenson, Adlai 22
Stevenson, Robert Louis . . . .
    20

Stockbrokers 233
Success 234
Swedish 116
Teamwork 236
Tennis 237
Tennyson, Alfred, Lord. . . . .
    207
Terence 173
Tex-Mex 228
Thackeray, William
    Makepeace 88
Thanksgiving 238
Thoreau, Henry David . . . .
    269
Thrift. 238
Travel. 60, 239
Troubles 234
Tusser, Thomas 64
Twain, Mark. . . 32, 135, 269
Vacation. 239
Valentine's Day 174,
    241
Van Dyke, Henry. 169
Victory. 241, 244
Virtue 242
Vos Savant, Marilyn . . . .
    239
Voss, John Henry 269
Wales. 243

War 244

Ward, Artemus 87

Wealth. 20, 140, 141,
142, 158, 231, 235, 244,
264

Weddings 30, 82, 150,
152, 153, 182, 188, 227,
229, 245

Welsh 12, 40, 50, 94,
118, 124, 229, 243

Wesley, John 50

West, Mae 179

Whittier, John Greenleaf
32

Wilde, Oscar. 13, 58,
60, 149, 155, 158

Willman, Marianne 53

Wilson, Earl. 239

Winchell, Walter 103

Wine and Spirits. 39,
85, 87, 89, 104, 107, 114,
155, 178, 256, 263, 268

Wisdom 262, 265

Wives 245, 254, 264

Women 265

Work 269

Writers and Writing 270

Yeats, William Butler . . . . . .
81, 262

Yorkshire. 97

Jennifer Rahel Conover comes from a family of diplomats and politicians. Her maternal grandfather, the Honorable Joseph E. Davies, was ambassador to both Russia and Belgium and his wife, legendary cereal heiress Marjorie Merriweather Post, was her step-grandmother. She has worked as a high-fashion model, an interior designer (for President Nixon's Winter White House), and with her husband, Ted, in the yacht charter business. Currently an award-winning photojournalist specializing in travel and yachting, she is published regularly in magazines, newspapers, and in-flight magazines throughout the world. She lives in South Florida with her husband and their Ragdoll cat, Kat . . . mandu. Her Web site is *www.toasts.org*.

Do you have a really great toast? Readers are welcome to submit their own toasts for possible inclusion in an upcoming work. Read and sign below (or on a photocopy) and return with your original toasts to:

Jennifer Rahel Conover
P.O. Box 4675
Fort Lauderdale, FL 33338

Your toast is:

In submitting your original toast, you represent that you are the author of the toast, and grant permission to Jennifer Rahel Conover, Penguin Putnam Inc. and their licensees, successors and assigns to include the toast, without fee, in all editions and derivations of an upcoming work, and in the advertising and promotion thereof in all media. You represent that you are the sole owner of the rights granted herein, and that your toast does not infringe upon the copyright, privacy right or other rights of anyone.

_____   _____
Signature   Print Name

_____
Date